LANDSCAPE PAINTING
Durand | Harrison

LANDSCAPE PAINTING

ASHER B. DURAND
BIRGE HARRISON

Velatura Press LLC, Publisher   Minneapolis, Minnesota USA

Landscape Painting: Asher B. Durand and Birge Harrison

Letters on Landscape Painting by Asher B. Durand
Original copyright 1855 by Asher B. Durand
The letters appeared in *The Crayon* between January and July, 1855.

Landscape Painting by Birge Harrison
Original copyright 1909 by Charles Scribner's Sons
Published in October, 1909.

Combined and edited by Darren R. Rousar

Current combined reprint edition published in 2013 by
Velatura Press, LLC
Minneapolis, Minnesota USA
www.velaturapress.com | www.studiorousar.com

Copyright ©2013 by Darren R. Rousar

ISBN-13: 978-0-9800454-5-1
ISBN-10: 0-9800454-5-2
First Printing, 2013
Printed in the United States of America

Cover art:
George Inness, *Spring Blossoms, Montclair, New Jersey* (detail), 1891

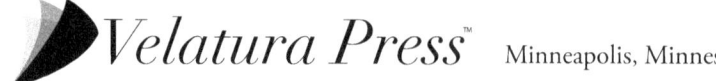 *Velatura Press*™ Minneapolis, Minnesota USA

For my wife, Kathleen

·Table Of Contents·

Introduction

The Hudson River School and the Tonalist Movement are two great periods in American landscape painting. They are oftentimes referred to as being distinctly American, although both periods had their roots in Europe. Many of America's famous artists, like Frederic Church, Asher Durand, George Inness and James Whistler, were part of one of these movements. Beyond the examples of their paintings, we are fortunate to have what I consider to be each movements textbooks.

In 1855, Asher B. Durand (1796-1886), a leading painter of the Hudson River School, wrote a series of nine articles for *The Crayon*, his son's art periodical. The articles, known as letters, were to be read as a response to a number of enquiries from would-be students. Durand claimed to not have the time to teach them and that, in any case, his tutelage would be of little use to the student. He cites his own lack of education as evidence for the latter. Of course Durand did have training, although perhaps not the kind for which students sought him. He was trained as an engraver, a profession which demands great draftsmanship and accuracy. Furthermore, he was good friends with, and a sketching companion of, Thomas Cole, the founder of the Hudson River School.

There are perhaps two overriding themes in Durand's nine letters: that Nature is a visual representation of God's truth, and that a true painting is built up from a number of smaller studies which were to be done directly from Nature.

Connecting God – to nature – to art, was nothing new. In fact Dante said as much in the thirteenth century, "*La natura e l'arte di Dio.*" – Nature is the art of God. Later, in the seventeenth century, Sir Thomas Browne expands on Dante's statement a bit, "*Now nature is not at variance with art, nor art with nature; they being both the servants of His providence. Art is the perfection of nature. Were the world now as it was the sixth day, there were yet a chaos. Nature hath made one world, and art another. In brief, all things are artificial; for nature is the art of God.*"

The eighteenth century English, *jack of all art-related trades*, John Ruskin, took this line of thinking into arts education. Durand's reading of Ruskin's *Modern Painters* likely helped codify his own thoughts about religion and art and as such may well have been the precursor to his *Letters On Landscape Painting*.

It is clear that Durand did not hide his light under a bushel. But whatever the reader's religious preference, there is much to be learned about landscape painting in his letters.

In the early 1900s, L. Birge Harrison (1854-1929), a prominent figure in the American Tonalist movement and a director of the Art Students' League's landscape school, gave a series of lectures at the League's summer school in Woodstock, New York. He later compiled those twenty-one lectures into the book, *Landscape Painting*.

Harrison's initial education was at the Pennsylvania Academy of the Fine Arts. John Singer Sargent later advised him to go to Paris, to study with Carolus-Duran, Sargent's former teacher. He was influenced by the Barbizon painters, a movement that had just been eclipsed by the Impressionists.

Like Durand before him, Harrison directs the student to nature. Despite, or perhaps because of its Tonalist outlook, *Landscape Painting*, has become a standard reference for many a plein air landscape painter. Even though Harrison's lectures were given to students of landscape painting, there is a wealth of information in them about representational painting and seeing in general. Many of his comments and directions will also be useful to students of still life, portrait and figure painting.

Although the Hudson River School and the Tonalists had different goals, they would agree in a number of areas. The following was written by Harrison, "*Take my word for it, technique is not the difficult thing in art. Any reasonably capable youth can readily master all of the technical problems in existence in a few short months, but it requires many a long and weary year to learn to see.*"* Durand said much the same thing in Letter I of his *Letters on Landscape Painting*.

This volume presents Durand's and Harrison's writings together for the first time. We will never know what they might have thought of their words being combined in such a way, but where they would disagree lay in the specifics of what makes each movement its own. Over the years hundreds of budding landscape painters and professionals alike have found value in these writings. It only seems fitting that the *textbooks* of two of America's great landscape painting movements be made available as a single work.

Most of the text is identical to the originals and very few changes have been made. The spelling, punctuation and grammar, current in 1855 and 1910, has been left largely intact. This includes the prevalence of hyphens and dashes, as well as the punctuation within sentences. Italicized text was generally in the originals.

Durand's *Letters* had no images in them but we have added some in this volume. Many of the original images Harrison chose were of night scenes. As such they are quite dark and did not reproduce well, even in the original. The images reproduced in this volume were scanned directly from a copy of the original 1910 edition and therefore suffer multi-generational losses. This loss is all the more obvious when using print-on-demand.

*See page 132 in this volume.

-Darren R. Rousar, 2013

LETTERS ON LANDSCAPE PAINTING

BY
ASHER BROWN DURAND

EDITED FROM THE ORIGINAL,
AS PUBLISHED IN THE CRAYON
JANUARY 1855 - JULY 1855

NEW YORK
W.J. STILLMAN AND J. DURAND
1855

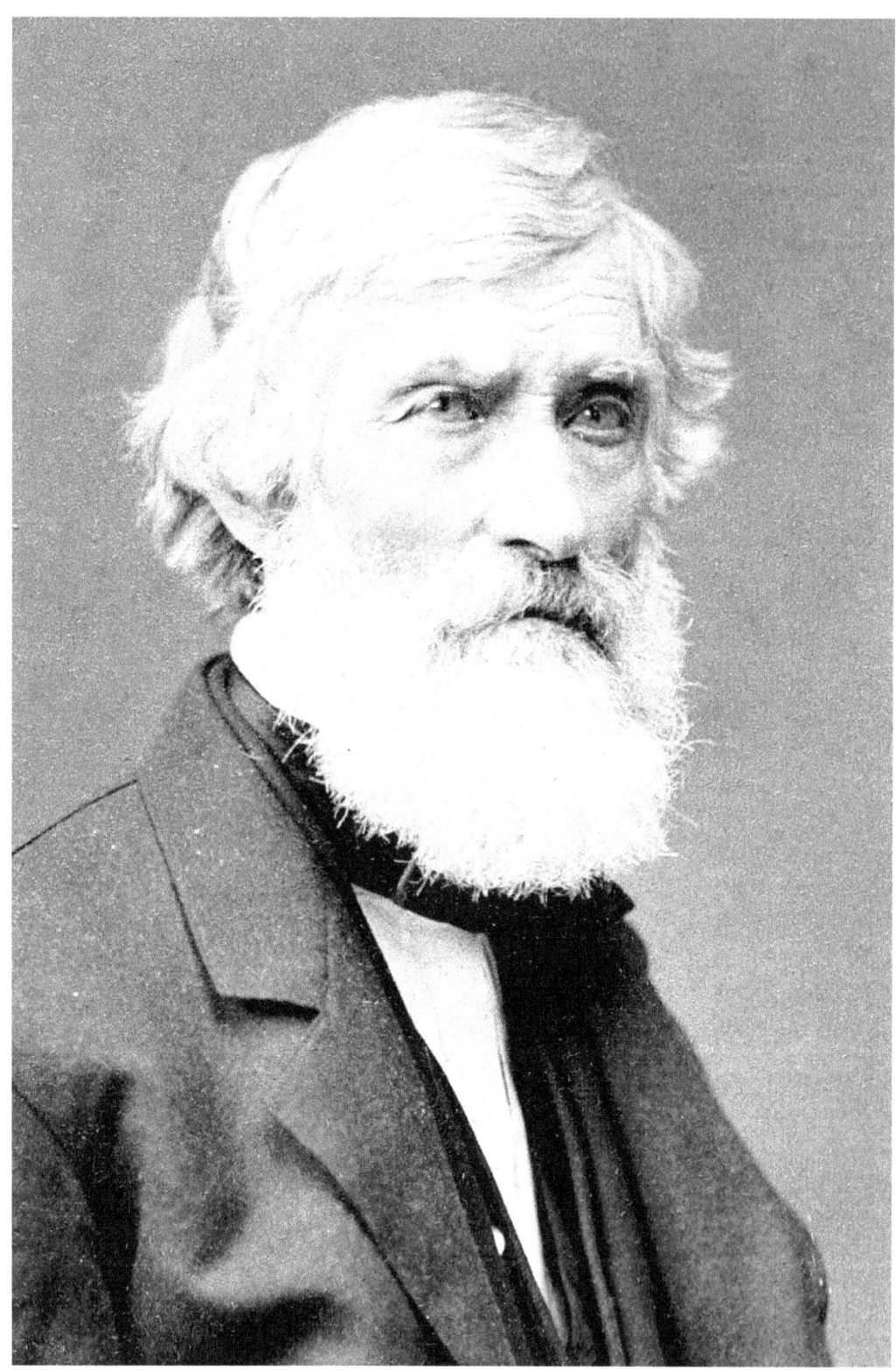

Asher B. Durand, 1869

Letters on Landscape Painting
Letter I

Dear Sir,

I am compelled to return an unfavorable answer to your application for admission into my studio as a pupil. Among the many instances in which I have found it necessary to return a refusal, your own case is most painful to me, on account of the earnest love of nature which you manifest, and the strong desire you have expressed to devote your whole time and energies to the study of Landscape Art.

I hope the disappointment will not be regarded by you as discouraging, for I can readily imagine you may have overestimated the advantage of such lessons as you desire at my hands, and I take occasion to submit for your consideration, by way of encouragement, some remarks, resulting from my own experience under circumstances very similar to your own. With the same *love* of beautiful nature from my childhood, and the corresponding desire for *its* development through the knowledge and practice of Art, I was, by several years, older than yourself before I was able to devote even a small portion of my time to the favorite pursuit. I then thought as you now think, that if I could but obtain a few lessons by seeing an experienced artist work, or working myself under his eye and direct instructions, most happy should I be. That privilege, however, I never enjoyed, and subsequent years of toil and study have somewhat modified my estimate of the value of such privileges. Indeed, I am almost certain that instead of any great final benefit resulting from it, the greater chance is, that in most instances its result will prove pernicious.

It is true that the pupil may thus save time in the acquisition of certain technical knowledge, mechanical processes, most suitable colors, etc., etc., at the same time, he is, at least, in danger of losing his own identity, and from the habit of seeing with the eyes and following in the track of his master, become in the end what is most degrading in the mind of every true artist, a mere imitator, a mannerist.

You need not a period of pupilage in an artist's studio to learn to paint; books and the casual intercourse with artists, accessible to every respectable young student, will furnish you with all the essential mechanism of the art. I suppose that you possess the necessary knowledge of drawing, and can readily express with the lead pencil the forms and general character of real objects. Then, let me earnestly recommend to you one Studio which you may freely enter, and receive in liberal measure the most sure and safe instruction ever meted to any pupil, provided you possess a common share of that truthful perception, which God gives to every true and faithful artist – the Studio of Nature.

Yes! go first to Nature to learn to paint landscape, and when you shall have learnt to imitate her, you may then study the pictures of great artists with benefit. They will aid you in the acquirement of the knowledge requisite to apply to the best advantage the skill you possess – to select, combine and set off the varied beauty of nature by means of what, in artistic language, is called treatment, management, etc., etc. I would urge on any young student in landscape painting, the importance of painting direct from Nature as soon as he shall have acquired the first rudiments of Art. If he is imbued with the true spirit to appreciate and enjoy the contemplation of her loveliness, he will approach her with veneration, and find in the conscientious study of her beauties all the great first principles of Art. Let him scrupulously accept *whatever* she presents him, until he shall, in a degree, have become intimate with her infinity, and then he may approach her on more familiar terms, even venturing to choose and reject some portions of her unbounded wealth; but never let him profane her sacredness by a willful departure from truth. It is for this reason that I would see you impressed, imbued to the full with *her* principles and practice, and after that develop the principles and practice of Art; in other words, the application of those phenomena most expressive of the requisite sentiment or feeling. For I maintain that all Art is unworthy and vicious which is at variance with Truth, and that only is worthy and elevated which impresses us with the same feelings and emotions that we experience in the presence of the Reality. True Art teaches the use of the embellishments which Nature herself furnishes, it never creates them. All the fascination of treatment in light, and dark, and color, are seen in Nature; they are the luxuries of her store-house, and must be used with intelligence and discrimination to be wholesome and invigorating. If abused and adulterated by the poisons of conventionalism, the result will be the corruption of, veneration for, and faith in, the simple truths of Nature, which constitute the true Religion of Art, and the only safeguard against the inroads of heretical conventionalism. If you should ask me to define conventionalism, I should say that it is the substitution of an easily expressed falsehood for a difficult truth.

But why discuss this point – is it not a truism admitted by all? Far from it! Or if it be admitted as a principle, it is constantly violated by the artist in his practice, and this violation sanctioned by the "learned" critic and connoisseur. The fresh green of summer must be muddled with brown; the pure blue of the clear sky, and the palpitating azure of distant mountains, deadened with lifeless grey, while the grey un-sheltered rocks must be warmed up and clothed with the lichens of their forest brethren – tricks of impasto, or transparency without character – vacant breadth, and unmitigated darkness – fine qualities of color without local meaning, and many other perversions of truth are made objects of artistic study, to the death of all true feeling for Art, – and all this under the name of improvements on Nature! To obtain truthfulness is so much more difficult than to obtain the power of telling facile falsehoods, that one need not wonder that some delusive substitute occupies the place which Nature should hold in the artist's mind.

I have offered to you these remarks and opinions as the result of experience. I do not desire that my humble productions shall be regarded as the evidence of their correctness. I am more certain as to their aim in accordance with these opinions than in their successful attainment of that aim; and I will only add that neither their faults nor their merits are chargeable to any instructions received in the studios of artists, though many a useful lesson has been taught me by intercourse with professional brethren – even often from the student and the tyro. But by far my most valuable study has been

"Under the open sky" –

and there would I direct you to

"Go forth and listen
To Nature's teachings, while from all around the
Earth and her waters, and the depths of air,
Comes a still voice" –

a voice that no student can disregard with impunity, nor heed without joy and gladness – broken, it is true, too often by repeated failure, and by the conviction that the most successful transcripts that Art is able to produce must appear but abortions in her presence, and only tolerable when withdrawn and examined in the seclusion of the painting room.

There are, however, certain motives in Art which I am persuaded the young landscape painter may do well to consider with reference to directing his studies. These I will give you as opportunity offers, in some future letters.

Truly yours,
A. B. Durand

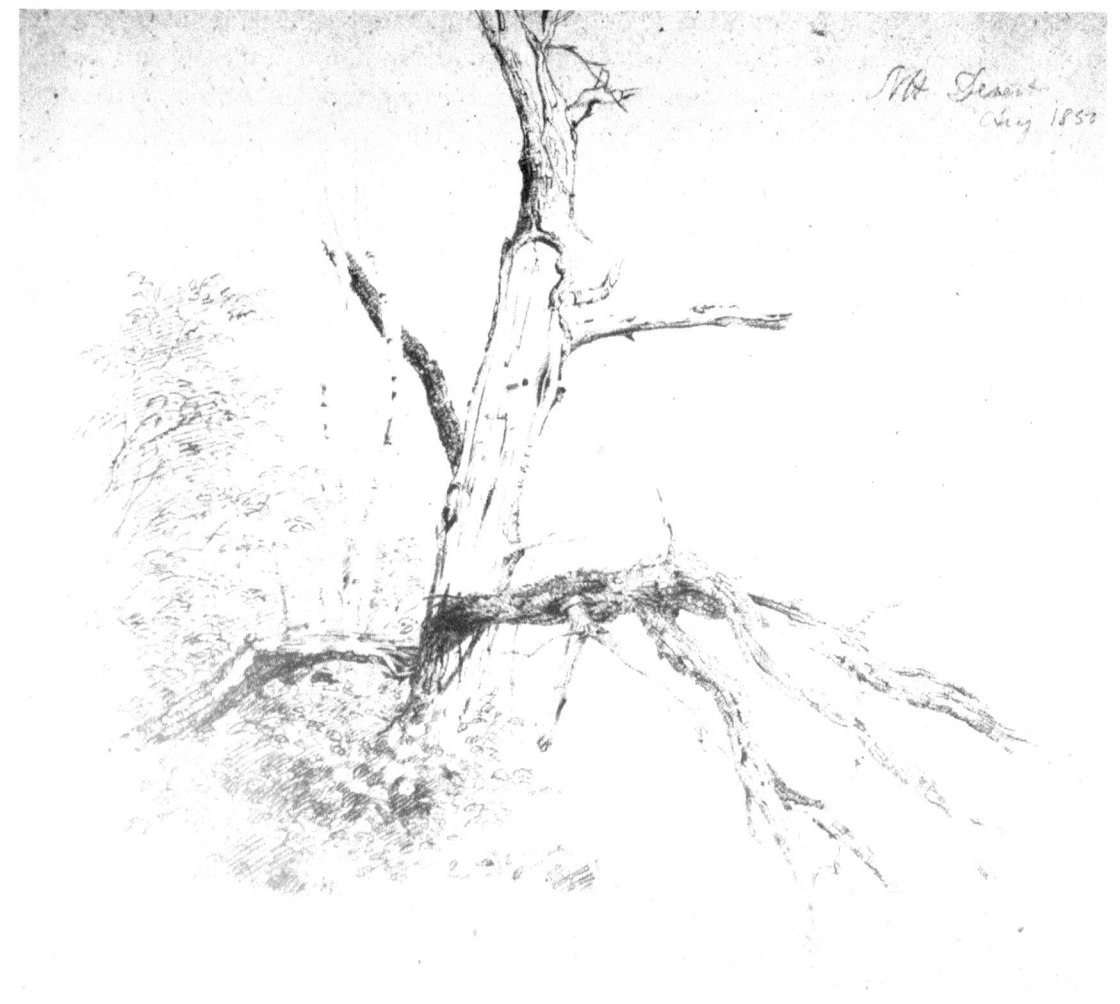

Study of a Tree - Mount Desert by Frederic Church, 1852

Letters on Landscape Painting
Letter II

Dear Sir,

In recommending you, in the beginning of your studies, directly to Nature, 1 would not deceive you with the expectation, that you will thus most speedily acquire the art of picture-making – that is much sooner acquired in the studio or the picture gallery.

I refer you to Nature early, that you may receive your first impressions of beauty and sublimity, unmingled with the superstitions of Art – for Art has its superstitions as well as religion – *that* you may learn to paint with intelligence and sincerity – that your works shall address themselves to intelligent and sympathetic minds, and spare you the mortification of ever seeing them allotted to swell the lumber of the garret and the auction room.

Form is the first subject to engage your attention. Take pencil and paper, not the palette and brushes, and draw with scrupulous fidelity the outline or contour of such objects as you shall select, and, so far as your judgment goes, choose the most beautiful or characteristic of its kind. If your subject be a tree, observe particularly wherein it differs from those of other species; in the first place, the termination of its foliage, best seen when relieved on the sky, whether pointed or rounded, drooping or springing upward, etc., etc.; next mark the character of its trunk and branches, the manner in which the latter shoot off from the parent stem, their direction, curves, and angles. Every kind of tree has its traits of individuality – some kinds assimilate, others differ widely – with careful attention, these peculiarities are easily learned, and so, in a greater or less degree, with all other objects. By this course you will also obtain the knowledge of that natural variety of form, so essential to protect you against frequent repetition and monotony. A moment's reflection will convince you of the vital importance of drawing, and the continual demand for its exercise in the practice of outline, before you begin to paint.

I know you will regard this at first thought as an unnecessary restriction, and become impatient to use the brush, under the persuasion that you can with it make out your forms, and at the same time produce color, and light, and shade. In this you deceive yourself – as many others have done, till the consequent evil has become irremediable, for slovenly and imperfect drawing finds but a miserable compensation in the palpable efforts to disguise or atone for it, by the blandishments of color and effect.

Practice drawing with the pencil till you are sure of your hand, and not only that, – till you shall have learned by heart the characteristic forms of all objects, animals, and the human figure included, so far as you may require their use in pictures; no matter how long it takes, it will be time gained. You will say that I impose on you a difficult and painful task: difficult it is, but not painful nor ungrateful, and let me assure you that its faithful performance is accompanied by many enjoyments that experience only can enable you to appreciate. Every step of conscious progress that you make, every successful transcript of the chosen subject, will send a thrill of pleasure to your heart, that you will acknowledge to give you the full measure of compensation.

As a motive to meet with courage and perseverance every difficulty in the progress of your studies, and patiently to endure the frequent discouragements attending your failures and imperfect efforts, so long as your love for Nature is strong and earnest, keeping steadily in view the high mission of the Art you have chosen, I can promise you that the time will come when you will recall the period of these faithful struggles with a more vivid enjoyment than that which accompanies the old man's recollections of happy childhood. The humblest scenes of your successful labors will become hallowed ground to which, in memory at least, you will make many a joyous pilgrimage, and, like Rosseau, in the fullness of your emotions, kiss the very earth that bore the print of your oft-repeated footsteps.

There is yet another motive for referring you to the study of Nature early – its influence on the mind and heart. The external appearance of this our dwelling-place, apart from its wondrous structure and functions that minister to our well-being, is fraught with lessons of high and holy meaning, only surpassed by the light of Revelation. It is impossible to contemplate with right-minded, reverent feeling, its inexpressible beauty and grandeur, forever assuming new forms of impressiveness under the varying phases of cloud and sunshine, time and season, without arriving at the conviction

– "That all which we behold
Is full of blessings" –

that the Great Designer of these glorious pictures has placed them before us as types of the Divine attributes, and we insensibly, as it were, in our daily contemplations,

– "To the beautiful order of his works,
Learn to conform the order of our lives."

Thus regarding the objects of your study, the intellect and feelings become elevated and purified, and in proportion as you acquire executive skill, your productions will, unawares, be imbued with that undefinable quality recognized as sentiment or expression which distinguishes the true landscape from the mere sensual and *striking* picture.

Thus far I have deemed it well to abstain from much practical detail in the pursuit of our subject, preferring first to impress you with a sense of the elevated character of the Art, which a just estimate of its capacity and purposes discloses, and this course may still be extended in reference to the wide field for its exercise, which lies open before you. If it be true – and it appears to be demonstrated, so far as English scenery is concerned – that Constable was correct when he affirmed that there was yet room for a natural landscape painter, it is more especially true in reference to our own scenery; for although much has been done, and well done, by the gifted Cole and others, much more remains to do. Go not abroad then in search of material for the exercise of your pencil, while the virgin charms of our native land have claims on your deepest affections. Many are the flowers in our untrodden wilds that have blushed too long unseen, and their original freshness will reward your research with a higher and purer satisfaction, than appertains to the display of the most brilliant exotic. The "lone and tranquil" lakes embosomed in ancient forests, that abound in our wild districts, the unshorn mountains surrounding them with their richly-textured covering, the ocean prairies of the West, and many other forms of Nature yet spared from the pollutions of civilization, afford a guarantee for a reputation of originality that you may elsewhere long seek and find not.

I desire not to limit the universality of the Art, or require that the artist shall sacrifice aught to patriotism; but, untrammeled as he is, and free from academic or other restraints by virtue of his position, why should not the American landscape painter, in accordance with the principle of self-government, boldly originate a high and independent style, based on his native resources, ever cherishing an abiding faith that the time is not far remote when his beloved Art will stand out amid the scenery of his "own green forest land," wearing as fair a coronal as ever graced a brow "in that Old World beyond the deep."

Truly yours,
A. B. Durand

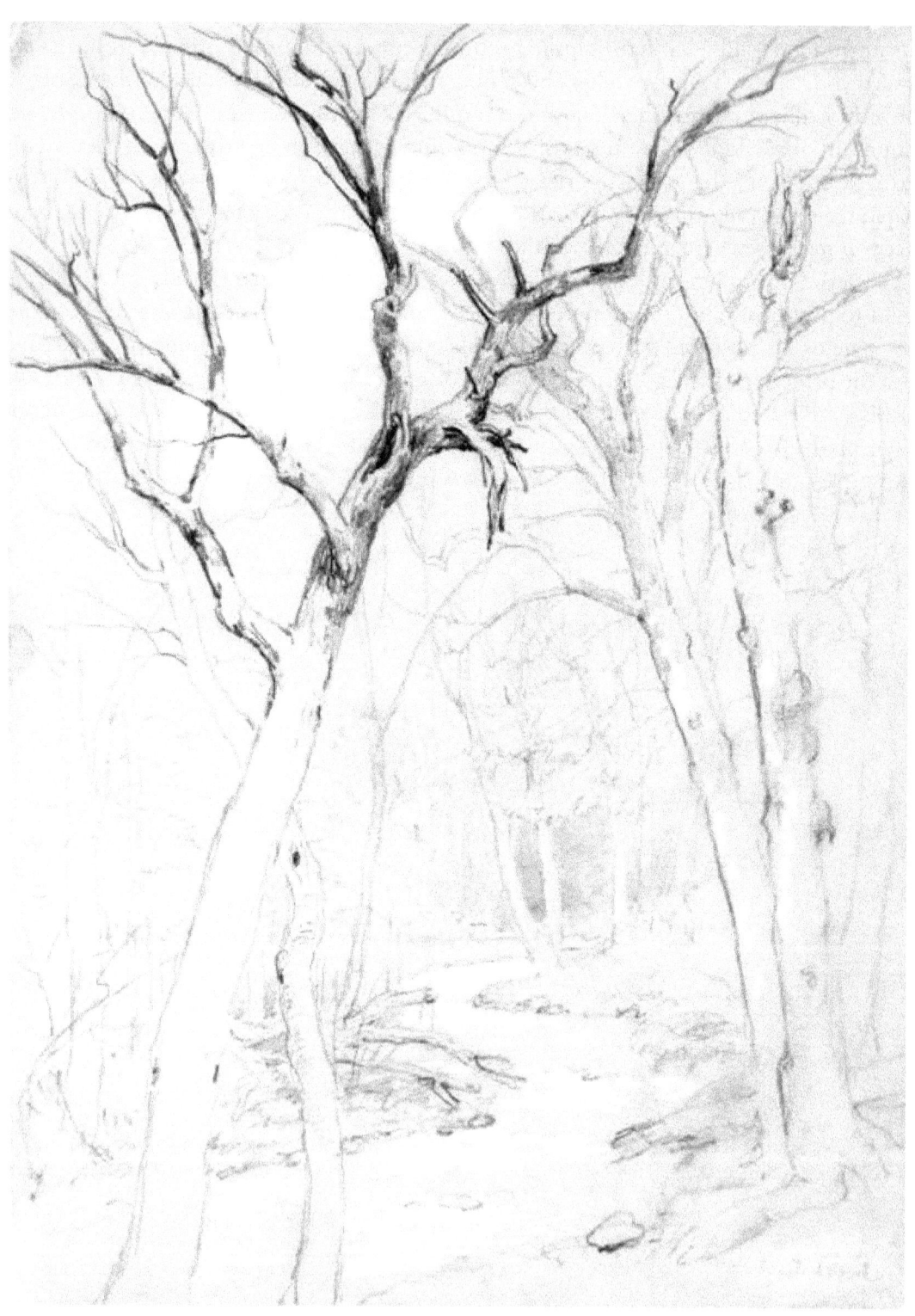

A Brook in the Woods by Asher B. Durand, 1854

Letters on Landscape Painting
Letter III

Dear Sir,

If a truly fine picture could be produced with the same certainty as an ordinary steam engine, specific directions might be given with a uniform result; and it would appear that thousands of landscapes *are* produced on precisely similar grounds, with even fewer claims to attributes of Fine Art. Although there are certain principles which constantly guide the hand of the true artist, which can be defined, classified, and clearly understood, and, therefore, communicable – yet the whole history of Art from the beginning, does not present a single instance where a thorough and scientific knowledge of these principles has of itself been able to produce a truly great artist, for the simple reason that such knowledge never can create the feeling, which overrules all principles, and gives the impress of true greatness.

I caution you, therefore, against reliance on any theoretical or technical directions which I or anyone else may give in the course of your studies, further than as means which you are to employ subject to your own feeling. It has not been my intention in these letters to show you *how* to paint so much as *what* to paint: to point out the distant object, and erect an occasional guide-board on what seems to me the best path leading to it. The means and modes of travel are already to be had at every roadside, and better than I can furnish. All that I might say on the various colors and mediums, tools, or whatnot, necessary for your purpose, including dissertations on design, composition, effect, color and execution, would only be a repetition of what has been already written and published throughout the land, and which you can readily procure of the colorman and the bookseller. After all whatever valuable instructions *they* furnish, their practical value must depend on your experience. All that I would advise is this – let materials be few and simple at first; as you advance, you will add what your feeling calls for. Much useful information may be obtained on all the subjects above mentioned, and you may be enlightened in the elements of *picturesqueness*, and other externals, with which alone too many artists, critics and connoisseurs, are contented; but those who can appreciate the higher attributes which make a picture a noble work of Art, will tell you that all the above-named requisites may be very imperfectly employed, and yet the picture may be truly fine, and even great; they will tell you that the difference consists in that which distinguishes the versifier from the poet, and this is all it is essential to know.

That is a fine picture which at once takes possession of you – draws you into it – you traverse it – breathe its atmosphere – feel its sunshine, and you repose in its shade without thinking of its design or execution, effect or color. These are after considerations: there is poetry in such a landscape, however humble. It will be great in proportion as it declares the glory of God, by a representation of his works, and not of the works of man.

I appeal with due respect from the judgment of those who have yielded their noblest energies to the fascinations of the *picturesque*, giving preference to scenes in which man supplants his Creator, whether in the gorgeous city of domes and palaces, or in the mouldering ruins that testify of his "ever fading glory," beautiful indeed, and not without their moral, but do they not belong more to the service of the tourist and historian than to that of the *true* landscape artist?

Without further multiplying words, you will perceive the purport of these observations. There can be no dissent from the maxim, that a knowledge of integral parts is essential for the construction of a whole – that the alphabet must be understood before learning to spell, and the meaning of words before being able to read – not to admit this would be absurd; yet many a young artist goes to work in the face of an equal absurdity – filling a canvas just as an idle boy might fill a sheet of paper with unmeaning scrawls, occasionally hitting the form of a letter, and, perhaps, even a word, so that the whole mass, at a little distance, may have the semblance of writing; and so, after he has wasted sufficient materials to have served, by well-directed study, to effect the attainment of the knowledge he lacks, he feels this deficiency, and goes back, or more correctly speaking, takes the first step forward, and begins with his letters. You have learned these letters, and how to spell, in the practice of drawing, and you have found out the meaning of many words, but there are yet many more, with phrases and whole sentences to learn (and this, I myself, feel, in more than one sense, while writing to you), before you can write and entirely express your thoughts.

Proceed then, choosing the more simple foreground objects – a fragment of rock, or trunk of a tree; choose them when distinctly marked by strong light and shade, and thereby more readily comprehended; do not first attempt foliage or banks of mingled earth and grass; they are more difficult of imitation, which, as far as practicable, should be your purpose. Paint and repaint until you are *sure* the work *represents* the model – not that it merely resembles it. This purpose, that is, the study of foreground objects, is worthy whole years of labor; the process will improve your judgment, and develop your skill – and perception, thought, and ingenuity will be in constant exercise. Thus you will not merely have observed in the rock, the lines, angles, and texture, and in the tree trunk, the scoring or plainness of surface, which respectively characterizes them, but you will have acquired knowledge and skill applicable alike to every portion of the picture. In producing such an imitation, you will have learned to represent shape with solidity, projection, depression, and relief, nearness and distance, the cooperation of color with form, light and shade, and above all, you will have developed and strengthened your perception of the natural causes of all these results.

In the tree trunk, for example, and also in the rock – though less simple, and not as suitable for the present illustration – you see the application of perspective, and a demonstration of the law which governs the expression of space. When the light strikes on the trunk of an oak, on the side directly at right angles with your vision, the scoring lines nearest the eye and towards the shadowed sides, are strongest and sharpest, graduating in distinctness from the center outward, and each division of bark diminishes proportionately. Light and color conform to these changes, being most pure or positive in the nearest portions. The lesson on the shape or rotundity of this object is not the only one; you have the principle of that gradation in light and dark, and color, which begins at the foreground, and extends to the horizon. Thus every *truthful* study of near and simple objects will qualify you for the more difficult and complex; it is only thus you can learn to read the great book of Nature, to comprehend it, and eventually transcribe from its pages, and attach to the transcript your own commentaries.

There is the letter and the spirit in the true Scripture of Art, the former being tributary to the latter, but never overruling it. All the technicalities above named are but the language and the rhetoric which expresses and enforces the doctrine – not to be unworthily employed to embellish falsehood, or ascribe meaning to vacuity. As I have not proposed to teach you processes, neither have I aimed at methodical arrangement or direction, further than so much as appears indispensable to a right beginning, I desire you to pursue the road pointed out with all consistent freedom from restraint, adding only such restrictive and experimental advice as shall incidentally appear to me advantageous to you.

If you should have a predilection for color, you will be most likely, in your early stage of practice, to give it undue importance, to an extent that may impede your progress – that is, sacrifice higher qualities to its fascination. I know no better safeguard to this liability, than to remind you that a fine engraving gives us all the greatest essentials of a fine picture, and often a higher suggestiveness than the original it represents, and so often, a mere outline, because the imagination fills in the rest, according to our own ideas of truth in its completeness. But, for the present I would especially direct attention to the light and dark, which make up the effect of the engraving, being far more complete than the outline; in short, it lacks nothing but color, which, though mighty in its power, is nothing more than the eloquence of Nature employed for the fullest enforcement of her Truth – the great ideas are antecedent. Waste not your time, therefore, on *broad sketches* in color; such only can be useful to the mature artist, as suggestive rather than representative. You had better look at all objects more with reference to light and dark than color, but do not infer from this that I would depreciate the value of color, for it is of inestimable value. It is, however, a sort of humorsome sprite or good demon – often whimsical and difficult of control – at times exceedingly mischievous, spoiling many a good picture as if with mere malicious intent – but when experience shall have acquainted you with its tricks and its virtues, you will understand better the worth of its service. Study, then, the light and dark of objects in connection with color, keeping in mind, as far as practicable, the distinction I have indicated; and as I have recommended first the practice of outline with the pencil, so I would also enjoin the study of light and shade with pencil, sepia, or even charcoal – any material you can best manage for this end. I would not debar you, in the meantime, the luxury of painting, but let your time be divided between the two. Nor will this course be lacking in interest and pleasure.

The same may be said in relation to confinement to foreground studies, for a period, as above advised; for in the advanced state of practice in which I find myself and at an age when early attractions might be supposed to lose some portion of their freshness, I feel no abatement in the interest of these pursuits, and no amount of toil and fatigue can overbalance the benefits, either in consideration of utility or enjoyment.

Yours, truly,
A. B. Durand

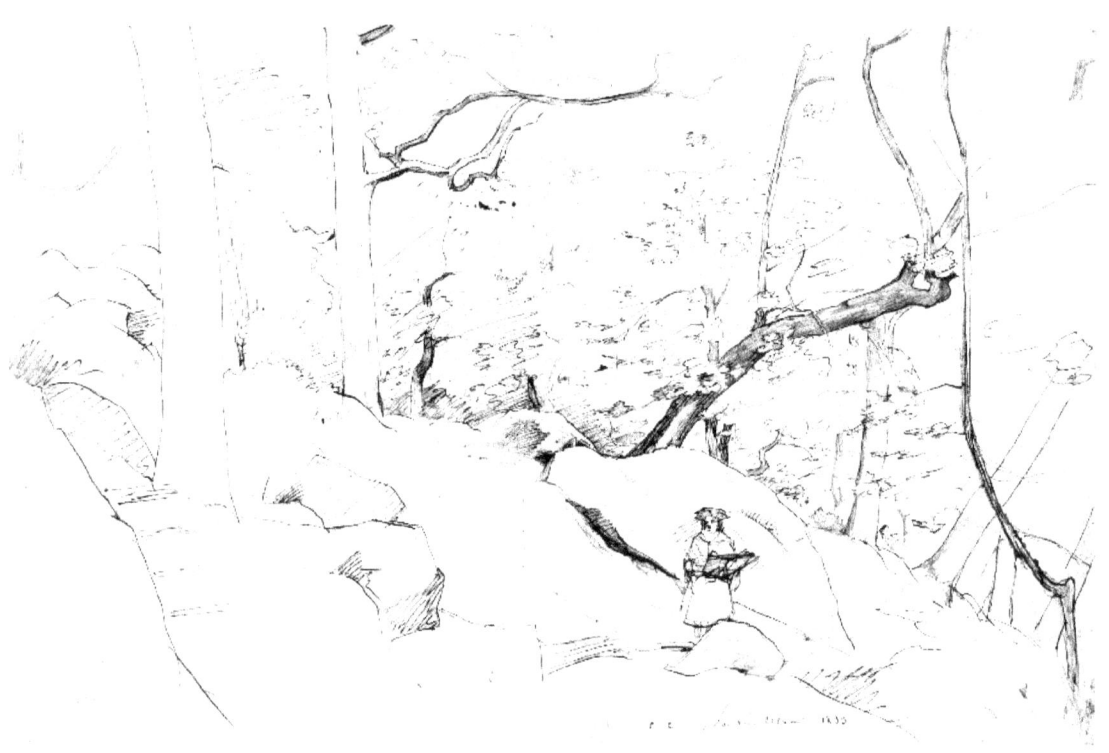

Painters Working in the Forests of Fontainebleau by Camille Corot, 1833

Letters on Landscape Painting
Letter IV

Dear Sir,

"You had better learn to make shoes," said the venerable Colonel Trumbull, one day, to a stripling who was consulting him in reference to his choice of painting as a profession, "better learn to make shoes or dig potatoes than to become a painter in this country." I felt that this was a harsh repulse to the young man, and most unexpected from such an authority. I was not then a painter, but secretly hoping to become one. I felt a strong sympathy for the victim, and thought he was unkindly treated, but I can now imagine that there might have appeared to the mind of the veteran artist sufficient ground for such advice, and that it may have been an act of kindness rather than severity. It is better to make shoes, or dig potatoes, or follow any other honest calling to secure a livelihood, than seek the pursuit of Art for the sake of gain. For whoever presumes to embrace her with the predominant motive of pecuniary reward, or any mere worldly distinction, will assuredly find but a bundle of reeds in his arms. The great law that provides for the sustenance of the soul through the ministry of spiritual things, has fixed an immovable barrier between its own pursuits and those which supply our physical wants. For this reason, we cannot serve God and mammon, however specious our garb of hypocrisy; and I would sooner look for figs on thistles than for the higher attributes of Art from one whose ruling motive in its pursuit is money. This is one of the principal causes operating to the degradation of Art, perverting it to the servility of a mere trade; and next to this, is its prostitution by means of excess in color, strong effects and skillful manipulation, solely for the sensuous gratification of the eye. Through such motives the Art becomes debased, and a picture so painted, be its subject landscape or figure, may well be considered but an empty decoration. But, fortunately for Art, such is not its true purpose, and it is only through the religious integrity of motive by which all real Artists have ever been actuated, that it still preserves its original purity, impressing the mind through the visible forms of material beauty, with a deep sense of the invisible and immaterial, for which end all this world's beauty and significance, beyond the few requirements of our animal nature, seems to be expressly given. And such is the verdict which the best judgment of the world, in all ages, has rendered, by awarding the highest rank to the artist who has kept in due subordination the more sensuous qualities with which material beauty is invested, thereby constituting his representation the clear exponent of that *intention*, by which every earnest spirit enjoys the assurance of our spiritual nature, and scorns the subtlety and logic of positive philosophy.

Every experienced artist knows that it is difficult to see nature truly; that for this end long practice is necessary. We see, yet perceive not, and it becomes necessary to cultivate our perception so as to comprehend the essence of the object seen. The poet sees in nature more than mere matter of fact, yet he does not see more than is there, nor what another may not see when he points it out. His is only a more perfect exercise of perception, just as the drapery of a fine statue is seen by the common eye, and pronounced beautiful, and the enlightened observer also pronounces it beautiful; but the one ascribes it to the graceful folding, the other to its expression of the figure beneath, but neither sees more nor less in quantity than the other, but with unequal degrees of completeness, in perception. Now, the highest beauty of this drapery consists in the perfection of its disposition, so as to best indicate the beautiful form it clothes, not possessing of itself too much attractiveness, nor lose its value by too strongly defining the figure. And so should we look on external Nature.

Why have the creations of Raphael conferred on him the title of *divine*? Because he saw through the sensuous veil, and embodied the spiritual beauty with which nature is animate, and in whose presence the baser "passions shrink and tremble, and are still." It is a mistake to suppose that Raphael and other earnest minds have added anything of their own to the perfection of their common model. They have only depicted it as they saw it, in its fullness and purity, looking on it with childlike affection and religious reverence, ever watchful that no careless or presumptuous touch should mar its fair proportions. And it is the same with regard to inanimate or animate creation. Childlike affection and religious reverence for the beauty that nature presents before us, form a basis of reliance which the conflicts of opinion can never disturb. Learn first to perceive with truthfulness, and then aim to embody your perceptions; take no thought on the question of genius or of future fame; with these you have nothing to do. Seek not to rival or surpass a brother artist, and above all, let not the love of money overleap the love of Art.

To appreciate Art, cultivation is necessary, but its power may be felt without that, and the feeling will educate itself into the desired appreciation, and derive from it a corresponding degree of pleasure, according to the purity or depravity, the high or low character, of the Art that awakens it. And, as the true and the beautiful are inseparably connected, and the highest beauty with the highest truth, it follows that the most truthful picture must be the most beautiful, according to the nature of its subject. Where is the portrait painter, having a just sense of his responsibilities, who has not often thrown down his brush in despair, after many fruitless attempts to express the soul that beams at times through the eye of beauty, and so with the yet more mysterious power of lofty intellect? And there is to be seen a corresponding soul and depth of expression in the beauty of landscape nature, which dignifies the Art that embodies it, and improves and elevates the mind that loves to contemplate its pictorial image.

But, suppose we look on a fine landscape simply as a thing of beauty – a source of innocent enjoyment in our leisure moments – a sensuous gratification with the least expenditure of thought or effort of the intellect, how much better is it than many a more expensive toy for which human skill and industry are tasked, and wealth continually lavished! How many of our men of fortune, whom nature and circumstance have well fitted for such enjoyment, surrender, as it were, their birthright, for a mess of pottage, by resorting to costly and needless luxuries, which consume, without satisfying – while Art invites to her feast of beauty, where indulgence never cloys, and entails no penalty of self-reproach!

To the rich merchant and capitalist, and to those whom even a competency has released from the great world-struggle, so far as to allow a little time to rest and reflect in, Landscape Art especially appeals – nor does it appeal in vain. There are some among "the innumerable caravan" that look to it as an oasis in the desert, and there are more who show signs of lively susceptibility to its refreshing influence – those who trace their first enjoyment of existence, in childhood and youth, with all the associations of their minority, to the country, to some pleasant landscape scenery; to such the instinct of nature thus briefly impressed, is seldom or never overcome. Witness the glad return of many an exile to the place of his nativity, and see the beautiful country-seat suddenly rising among the green trees that were young with himself, and almost regarded as playmates. He returns to end his days where they began, and loves to embellish the consecrated spot with filial tenderness, strewing fresh flowers on the grave of long departed years. To him who preserves the susceptibility to this instinctive impulse, in spite of the discordant clamor and conflict of the crowded city, the true landscape becomes a thing of more than outward beauty, or piece of furniture.

It becomes companionable, holding silent converse with the feelings, playful or pensive – and, at times, touching a chord that vibrates to the inmost recesses of the heart, yet with no unhealthy excitement, but soothing and strengthening to his best faculties. Suppose such an one, on his return home, after the completion of his daily task of drudgery – his dinner partaken, and himself disposed of in his favorite armchair, with one or more faithful landscapes before him, and making no greater effort than to look into the picture instead of on it, so as to perceive what it represents; in proportion as it is true and faithful, many a fair vision of forgotten days will animate the canvas, and lead him through the scene: pleasant reminiscences and grateful emotions will spring up at every stop, and care and anxiety will retire far behind him. If he possess aught of imaginative tissue, and few such natures are without it, he becomes absorbed in the picture – a gentle breeze fans his forehead, and he hears a distant rumbling; they come not from the canvas, but through the open window casement. No matter, they fall purified on his sensorium, and *that* is far away in the haunts of his boyhood – and that soft wind is chasing the trout stream down the woody glen, beyond which gleams "the deep and silent lake," where the wild deer seeks a fatal refuge. He shifts the scene, and stretching fields and green meadows meet his eye – in such he followed the plough and tossed the new mown hay; by the roadside stands the schoolhouse, and merry children scatter from its door – such was the place where he first imbibed the knowledge that the world was large and round, while ambition whispered that the village grounds were too narrow for him, – and with the last rays of the setting sun, the picture fades away.

I need scarcely apologize for the seeming sentimentalism of this letter. In this day the sentiment of Art is so overrun by the *technique*, that it can scarcely be insisted on too strongly. In my next, I shall recur more minutely to the means, rather than the ends, of Art.

Yours truly,
A. B. Durand

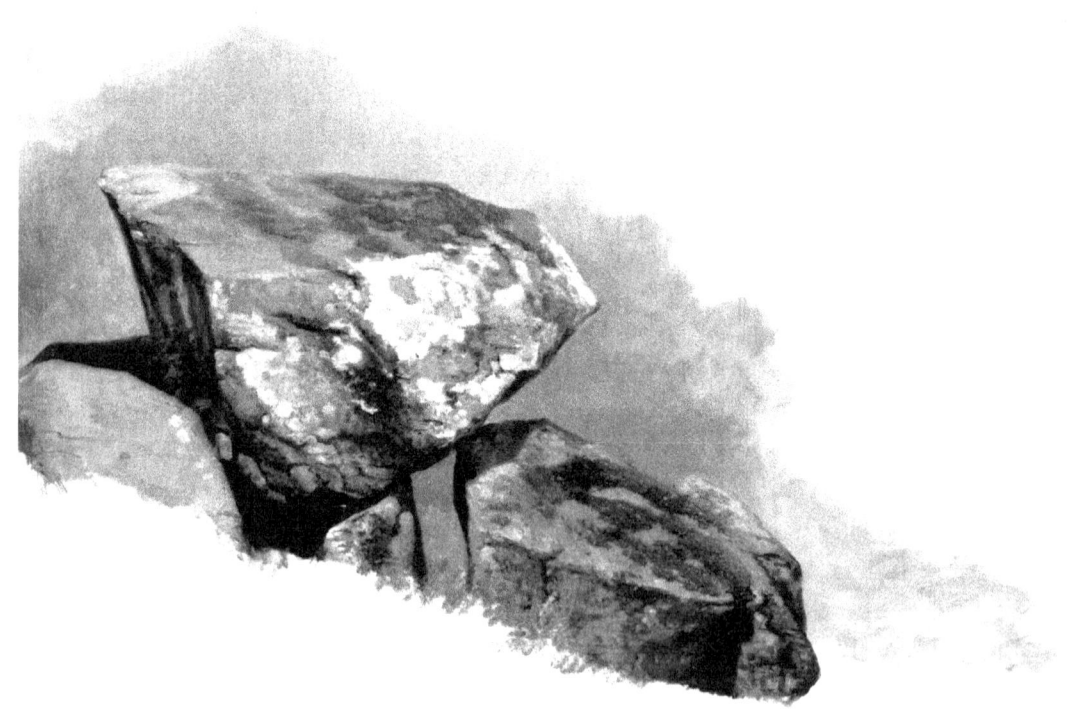

Study of a Rock by Asher B. Durand

Letters on Landscape Painting
Letter V

Dear Sir,

I have already advised you to aim at direct imitation, as far as possible, in your studies of foreground objects. You will be most successful in the more simple and solid materials, such as rocks and tree trunks, and after these, earth banks and the coarser kinds of grass, with mingling roots and plants, the larger leaves of which can be expressed with even botanical truthfulness; and they should be so rendered, but when you attempt masses of foliage or running water, anything like an equal degree of imitation becomes impracticable.

It should be your endeavor to attain as minute portraiture as possible of these objects, for although it may be impossible to produce an absolute imitation of them, the determined effort to do so will lead you to a knowledge of their subtlest truths and characteristics, and thus knowing thoroughly that which you paint, you are able the more readily to give all the facts essential to their *representation*. So this excessively minute painting is valuable, not so much for itself as for the knowledge and facility it leads to.

There is then a marked distinction between *imitation* and *representation*, and if this distinction be at first difficult to understand, it will become more and more apparent as you advance. Although painting is an imitative Art, its highest attainment is representative, that is, by the production of such resemblance as shall satisfy the mind that the entire meaning of the scene represented is given. Now, if all objects in Nature could be equally well imitated, there would be no need of this distinction; but this is not the case. Take a tree, for instance: with its infinity of leafage, you perceive at once that direct imitation is impossible; that is, such an imitation of its foliage as you produce of its trunk, or of the rock beneath, for to that effect each leaf must be defined as far as seen, or at least a great portion of them, and with the same precision with which you express the scoring of its trunk. You are then to *represent* this foliage in every essential characteristic, without defining the forms of individual leaves. To do this, some analysis of its structure is necessary. In the first place, it presents you with form, and mass, so far like a solid object, which it is not, and herein is your greatest difficulty; it is open and permeable, and in a measure transparent, so that you see its nearer surface, and through that to its central portions and opposite limit. If you attempt to portray it. by the usual process for rounded objects – its local color in the great mass of light and natural gradation into the shade of its receding surface – you will only have the effect of a solid object. You must do much more than this; the hue of the background on which it is relieved, must be seen through its apertures in some parts, in others the retiring color and texture of its center and opposite branches, together with gleams of reflection from the enlightened portions of its interior (for the light strikes through it, as well as on it); then its species must be determined by the form of its clusters, marking the divisions on its surface, and especially their terminations, or contour, which express its distinctive character. In addition to this, you are to observe the kind of texture which its leafage requires; also, reflections from the sky visible on the upper portions of the shaded side. When you shall have done all this, it is only representative, yet it satisfies the eye as fully as an imitation. Similar difficulties occur in painting near water. We see its surface: through that, the bottom, when shallow, and at the same time surrounding objects and the sky above, all distinctly imaged upon this surface; all attempt at imitation must fall far short, and yet water may be as unmistakably represented as trees.

Strictly speaking, beyond a few foreground objects, our Art is entirely representation, and that can be rendered satisfactory only by the utmost effort to produce imitation. When you shall have acquired some proficiency in foreground material, your next step should be the study of the influence of atmosphere – the power which defines and measures space – an intangible agent, visible, yet without that material substance which belongs to imitable objects, in fact, an absolute nothing, yet of mighty influence. It is that which above all other agencies, carries us into the picture, instead of allowing us to be detained in front of it; not the doorkeeper, but the grand usher and master of ceremonies, and conducting us through all the vestibules, chambers and secret recesses of the great mansion, explaining, on the way, the meaning and purposes of all that is visible, and satisfying us that all is in its proper place. This, therefore, is an important personage, and no pains should be spared to make his acquaintance.

Having become familiar with the *light* and *dark* of foreground objects, and their distinctness, fullness of detail, and freshness of color, place yourself so as to include a view of these with a gradually retiring distance. You will perceive that similar objects to those nearest you, at a few hundred yards distant, have undergone considerable change, and that change becoming more and more apparent with every step beyond. An examination into these changes affords us the first lesson in atmospheric space. First direct your attention to the *dark* portions of the scene, the shaded sides of objects, and the shadows cast by them on the ground and on each other. In the first place you will find these darks have lost something in strength, and not only are they weaker but less distinctly marked with details, and more negative in color, as if by the infusion of a bluish gray, scarcely perceptible at first, but more obvious further on. This invariably takes place at the first remove from the foreground, and must be carefully expressed, whether the eye discerns it or not, for it is a principle, (I have reference to objects seen in a clear day, all under the same conditions). At every remove, then, the darks become weaker and weaker, and their details or markings within them fainter and fainter.

I call your attention first to the darks, because their variations are more palpable and thorough, (especially in color) than those of the lights, but the latter also undergo material changes, gradually losing their details, becoming softer in texture, and weaker, though not so essentially changed, in color; till at length, when individual form is no longer distinguishable, the mingling light and dark are resolved into one mass of comparatively uniform color, as in the far distant mountain. The sum of all this is simply the natural gradation from darker to lighter, stronger to weaker, on a principle as fixed as the chromatic scale in music; and the practiced eye of the artist will detect the slightest discord in the one, as will the sensitive ear in the other. This will serve as a general guide to the effect of a clear atmosphere, bearing in mind that the upper portions of distant mountains are stronger and more defined than their bases, the air being more transparent in proportion to elevation.

You will observe that the open or permeable quality of trees is soon lost as you advance in the distance, and they partake more the appearance of solid objects, with the exceptions of the small openings or interstices which alone determine their looseness of structure. Water, also, presents nothing but surface, and its transparency is only observable by its reflections. Here note especially, that the clearness of distant water does not depend on the use of transparent color, but on the distinctness of reflections on its surface, and so all broad shadows, from whatever causes, owe their transparency to the precise sufficiency of their details, that is the right degree of distinctness with which objects within them are defined. We frequently see in pictures broad masses of transparent color applied to represent shadows, yet utterly void of clearness, in consequence of mere blankness, no objects being seen, or at least distinctly seen, within them.

To conclude these brief hints – atmosphere is, as you know, a veil or medium interposed between the eye and all visible objects – its final influence is to obscure and to equalize. It is *felt* in the foreground, *seen* beyond that, and *palpable* in the distance. It spreads over all objects the color which it receives from the sky in sunlight or cloudlight; and the only rule I can furnish you for the expression of its hue, is, that it partakes more and more the color of the sky. Thus far the expression of atmospheric space, according to the distance of objects from the foreground, is comparatively easy; but when considered under the influence of a variable sky, cloud shadows, and drifting vapor, it becomes more complex, and all the subtleties of light with color subject to the media through which it passes, and the intricacy of reflections from accidental causes, will engage your attention, and call in requisition all your powers of observation.

The degrees of clearness and density, scarcely two successive days the same – local conditions of temperature – dryness and moisture – and many other causes, render anything like specific direction impracticable. I can do little more than urge on you the constant study of its magic power, daily and hourly, in all its changes, at times shortening, at others lengthening, the space before you; now permitting to be defined, in all its ruggedness, the precipice on the mountain side – and now transforming it to a fairy palace, and the solid mountain itself to a film of opal.

I must allude to this subject further in other connections – its importance being too great to be passed by with a single consideration.

Yours, truly, A. B. Durand.

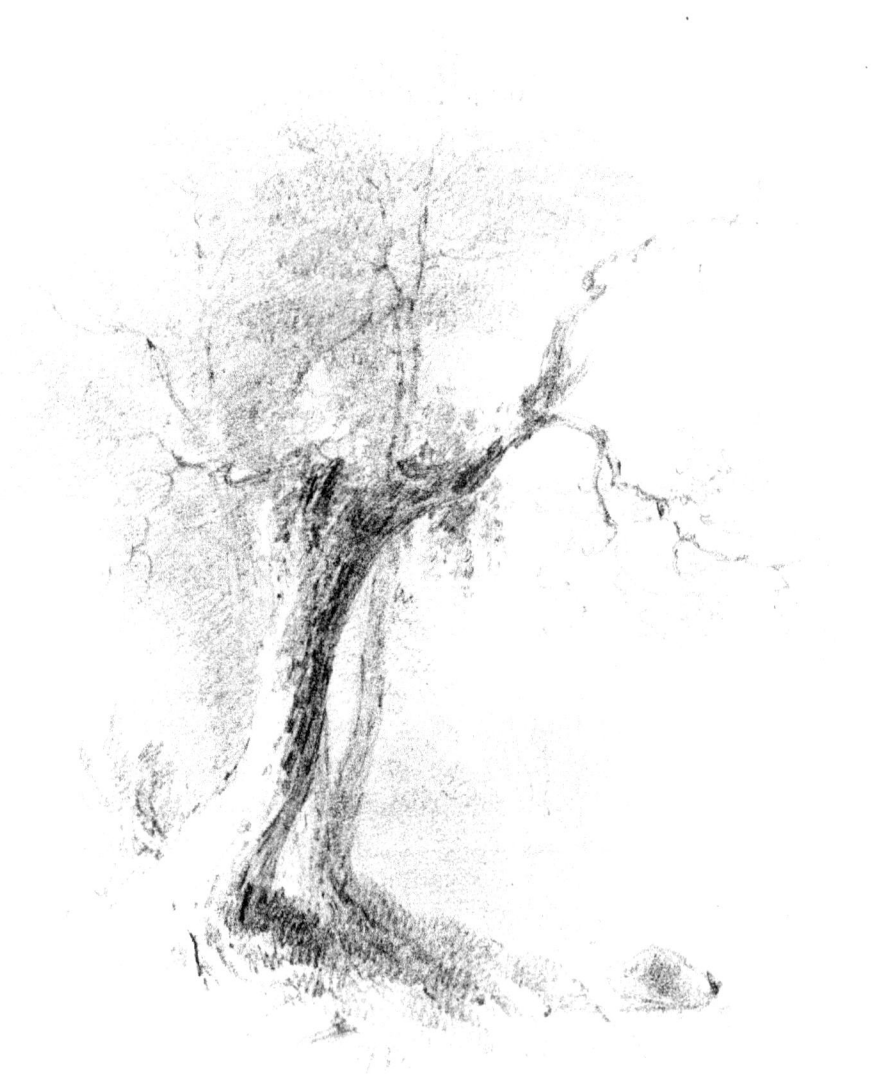

Tree Study by Asher B. Durand

Letters on Landscape Painting
Letter VI

Dear Sir,

In my last I threw out some hints on atmospheric gradation. It was there stated, as a principle, that this gradation was most apparent and invariable in the darks or shaded portions of the landscape, under a clear sky, such portions partaking more and more the color of the sky as they recede. The natural cause for this effect is the same as that which produces the blue of the sky – the intervention of the great body of atmosphere between the earth, and the utter darkness of surrounding space. A luminous, transparent white, spread over black, becomes blue in proportion to its purity; and, as the atmosphere is less pure near the earth, so the sky is less blue at the horizon, thence gradually increasing to the zenith. The blueness of the distant mountain and the intermediate gradation, are subject to this law.

It was also stated, in my last letter, that this regular gradation was interrupted, and the effect of atmosphere complicated, by the intervention of clouds and other vapors; but, previous to an examination of such phenomena, let us take into consideration the influence of sunlight.

Sunshine is the joyous expression of Nature, the lovely smile that lights up all her beauty, so changing and adorning all it rests upon, as to seem itself creative. Mingling with the fitful humors of the atmosphere, it develops the full power of color, and evolves the interminable variety of light and shade which constitutes the magic of chiaroscuro – that controlling element of effect which theorists have in vain endeavored to portion and systemize. Who does not feel that existence is a blessing and the world beautiful, when, after tedious days of sullen cloud and storm, and worse monotonous drizzle, suddenly the sun breaks forth in noonday splendor? So gladdening is his presence, that we forget at once the long gloom of his absence. And who, so well as the landscape artist, can appreciate such a change? And, having so often enjoyed its blessing, he would be most ungrateful and unworthy not to bear witness by his works to its surpassing loveliness. I have more respect for the devout heathen who worships the sun as the visible Divinity, than for the artist whose pictures betray insensibility to the charm of sunlight.

It is first declared by light and shade, but its full expression depends on color. Simple light may be represented without color, but sunshine never. Preparatory, therefore, to the few hints I shall give towards the representation of sunlight, I will call your attention to the general classification of the colors into the three divisions of warm, cold, and neutral. Reds and yellows form the basis of all warm color, and blue that of the cold – an equal admixture of the three forms the neutral. This division will serve our present purpose. And we learn from it that the color of sunlight is either red or yellow, or compounded of both, being warm, and that its absence or shade must present a predominance of blue, expressive of its coldness. And, however, little of positiveness may appear in these elements, either in the light or shade, there will always exist the marked distinction of warmth and coolness when compared. This is an invariable principle, or, if there be any exceptions, it is traceable to adventitious causes, such as those of strong reflections, which will be considered as we proceed.

All warm colors are enhanced or become more positive in sunlight, and all cold color loses something of its identity by the infusion of warmth; in other words, it has affinity for the warm, and antipathy for cold; it is, therefore, important to keep in view the quality of the color on which it falls.

The best time to observe the ordinary effect of sunshine on the landscape, is to watch the gradual clearing up of a cloudy day, when its presence is first announced by occasional patches of light. The first sensation conveyed is, of course, that of light – the next, that of color; the entire mass of such light being warm compared with the surrounding shade. Study the effect, first, in the middle distance, when a cloudy sky just begins to open and lets its first burst of sunlight in. You will find that around the light the shadow appears cooler, owing to the suddenness of contrast; but, as the openings overhead widen, the cold light from the clear blue sky is reflected into the shadow, and the entire mass of it becomes colder even to a greater degree than the unpracticed eye readily admits. So, if you should paint the scene with the utmost truth during a cloudy day, and afterwards introduce these patches of sunlight, the picture would be entirely false.

Your shadows would not only be too warm and positive in local color, but all forms within them too defined, inasmuch as sunlight always obscures the details of the adjoining shadows according to their magnitude – those of the broader masses remaining most distinct. The amount of warm color in sunshine is regulated by the hour of the day, and condition of the atmosphere, ordinarily the least at noon. Generally it contains more of yellow than red, but at times assuming every grade of golden orange and crimson, so that all attempts at any specific prescription must ever remain inadequate, whether artistic or scientific, and only useful so far as to direct the student, or even force him to entire reliance on his own powers of observation "under the open sky." For which end, I have assumed the task of advising you.

You will further observe, that all shadows cast from objects in direct sunlight have their edges sharply defined and strongest at their starting point (when no reflection is present). This is the first distinguishing difference between sunshine and ordinary daylight, under a cloudy sky. Any softening or blending of such shadow with the light must impair, if not destroy, its reality. Be careful to note the direction, length and breadth of shadows, according to the rules of perspective, and their adaptation to the surface on which they rest. And that all broad masses from clouds or other large bodies, are weaker than those of smaller dimensions, embracing, as they do, a greater amount of reflections from the sky and surrounding objects.

I have referred you to middle grounds and distance the better to discern the influence of sunlight, in reference to the color of shadows; but the same principles operate in foreground, though less palpable in this particular. You have here the contrasts of light and dark, warmth and coolness of color, the same sharpness of edges* and reflections from the sky, less influenced by the atmosphere, but still perceptible, and a proportionate indistinctness of detail, regulated by the magnitude of the shadow. In addition to these you find another agency employed of great value, that is, the force of strong reflections from contiguous objects at times materially affecting the quality of the color of the shadow. Whenever the sun's rays strike an object within the margin of a shadow, according as that object is elevated above the plane of the shadow, it will reflect those rays modified by its own color and peculiar surface, into the ground of the shadow, often giving positive warmth to its coolness, thus becoming the exception above mentioned to the principle I have laid down; so that when such shadow is very circumscribed, it becomes warm throughout, and even hot where the reflecting cause is very warm and glowing in color. The same action takes place to a limited extent, in more distant localities, though less conspicuous, as in the ravine of the middle ground, with its sunny and shaded sides, and the steep slopes of more distant elevations. In the midst of sunlight and its shadows, look out then for the sly agents of reflection, forever meddling with the sports of sunshine, whether among the pebbles by the brook-side, or the precipices of the mountain.

We are not liable to over-estimate the value of sunshine to the landscape. By it all beauty is rendered more beautiful, and the ungainly made attractive. Color, as we have seen, is dependent on it for its highest development, and chiaroscuro for its greatest charm. But, independent of its pictorial efficacy, it imparts a cheerful sentiment to the picture that all observers feel and enjoy; even the fearful darkness of storm and tempest is palliated and becomes agreeable, if but a gleam of sunshine enliven some corner of the scene; and, as it glides through the woven arches of the solemn forest, touching here and there some mossy trunk and pendant bough, and chequering the rich mould beneath with variegated gems, it cheers the silent gloom, and surprises us with the sudden presence of unlooked-for beauty.

The common prejudice against green landscapes seems to me to arise from the neglect of studying the effect of sunlight in varying the green, and as this is a prejudice as general among artists as injurious to our true perception of nature, I will give some space to the consideration of this part of our subject.

---

*Sharpness of the edges, or terminations of all foreground shadows, is, of course, dependent on the solidity or openness of the extremities of the object casting it. And all cloud shadows approaching the foreground, have soft terminations, so far differing from those of the distance; so the edges will be soft and the mass weak, in proportion to the remoteness of the object which cast it from the ground on which it falls, as those of hills or mountains, when such shadows cross the near middle ground.

In consequence of the prevalence of green in our summer landscape, the presence of sunlight becomes indispensable as the best means to counteract monotony. For Nature, indeed, abhors monotony as she does a vacuum, and perhaps it is to this feature above all others that we may ascribe the unpleasantness of a dull, cloudy day. I am inclined to believe that sleep would ensue from the contemplation of a surrounding mass of unvaried color, as soon as from the most somnorific monotony of sound or motion. In form, light and dark, and especially in color it is repulsive, and only admissible in the picture when necessary to the expression of a particular sentiment. But Nature, in this, as in all other cases, provides for the emergency. She is not only, generally, sparing in the employment of all strong positive color, but never permits a large unvaried mass of any single color. The local green of foliage, grass and plants, varies perpetually according to species and locality – tints of every shade, with mosses and lichens, diversify the surface of rocks – mineral and vegetable dyes mottle the bare earth, while water, in its transparency, mobility and mimic reflections, appropriating to itself the diversity of all; where, then, shall we look for monotony? Surely not in the sky, whose vault of graduated blue is forever changing, and in whose realm of clouds not even its semblance is permitted to enter.

I am free to confess, that my perception of Nature's beauty is not sufficiently sensitive to be wounded by the sunny green of summer – I cannot persuade myself that it is not beautiful, being, as it is, the first witness of organic life in the creation, the universal sign of unimpeded and healthy action; and, above all, the chosen color of creative Love for the earth's chief decoration. But I can well understand why it has been denounced by the Artist – it is the difficulty of its truthful representation – for it appears to me that no other color is attended with equal embarrassments. I am persuaded, therefore, that the prejudice against green pictures, or rather the supposed impracticability of all efforts to render them pleasing, arises more from failure to represent their greenness truly, than from any inherent objection. Who will assert that the fresh green of summer is not beautiful? Ever grateful to the sight, and soothing to the mind – the poet delights to revel in it, and the dusty eyes of the tired citizen regards it as a Godsend whenever permitted to enjoy it! Then why should the picture which represents it, be looked on as offensive? Alas, for the conventionalisms of Art!

If you paint a vast forest or extensive plains with one unvaried shade of green, it will indeed be repulsive, for Nature never does that: if you add to this the natural diversity of form and texture, with even truth of sunlight, you will still fall short of the mark; for, besides this, Nature has so varied her greens with an infinity of different shades, almost every tree even of the same kind differing from each other, that strictly speaking there is no monotony in *her* forests, and the same variety exists in the surface of her green fields – in the hues of the various grasses, and the tinting of numerous flowers.

But, notwithstanding this variety, large masses of green forests or extensive plains may be thought objectionable, from the requirement of a preponderance of green in your picture, thereby tending to dullness, but let the golden sunshine fall on given portions, and the sea of emerald will at once become redolent with life and beauty, and in proportion to the true expression of the light, especially in relation to the variety of local tints within it, and accompanied by a suitable use of cloud-shadows, all objectionable monotony and undue preponderance of positive green, will at once disappear – still more will this be the result when occurring under the condition of a soft atmosphere, neutralizing more sensibly the greenness of the receding part.

The chief difficulty in the management of green is found in the painting of trees, and on this point I desire to make a few more remarks. We find no green thing in Nature of sufficient magnitude to be conspicuous that has not inequality of surface, or that is not so fashioned as to prevent anything like an equal distribution of light at the same time over its entire surface. The leaves of all large plants are waving or undulating, or multiform in structure. And the tree, the largest and most abundant of all objects that bear the color, is most varied by irregularities of all shapes and dimensions; loosely composed in all its parts, and textured in every degree of depression and projection, the entire surface is a labyrinth of inequalities, so that it would appear a special provision of Nature to guard against the remotest liability to sameness or monotony of color on its surface, either singly observed, or when grouped in the mighty forest.

For this inequality and looseness of surface, with its irregularly rounded form, precludes the possibility of exposure to the same angle, and more especially to the reception of an equal quantity of light at the same time, on any considerable portion, and every variation in this respect presents a difference of color or varying shade of its green; so that on close examination you will find that the green proper, or actual color of the tree, is confined to the central portion of the light side where the sunshine falls, and all the rest is more or less negative, the shaded side, as a mass, scarcely green at all. This results from the looseness of structure, for it would be much more green were it a solid object, because the sun's rays penetrate its substance, and some portions of them pass to the opposite extremity, as I have previously reminded you. This neutrality of the shade is explained by the law which governs the color of light in its passage through semi-transparent bodies, becoming warmer and warmer, at first more orange, and as the medium becomes denser, finally red; for example, if you look at a leaf in sunlight you will find the upper, or side on which the light falls, a cool green, while the under side will be a warm green inclining to orange. This transmitted light, falling in its turn as direct light on still other leaves, is still further warmed by the same influence, and thus partially neutralizes the actual color of the foliage by mingling its opposing color with it.** Thus the shadows of a tree are more nearly neutral than those of a solid substance of the same color, and if represented as green will be at once false and consequently offensive.

Yours truly,
A. B. Durand

** You may illustrate this further by letting a single ray of light into a close apartment, and then holding a thin sheet of some semi-transparent substance over the aperture. The light will receive a warm tinge, increasing in warmth with each layer of the substance added, until it finally becomes a deep red. –See Goethe on Color.

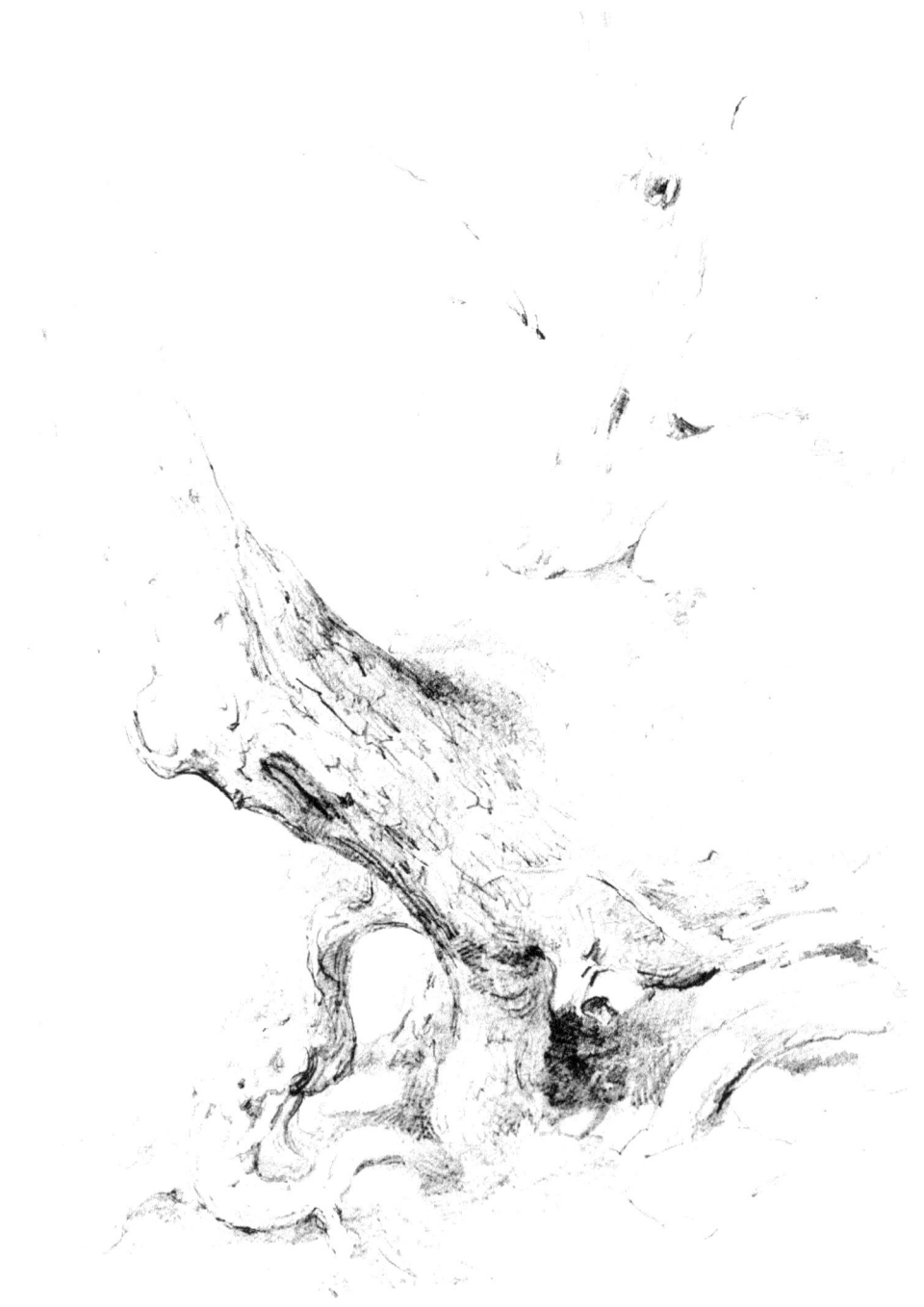

Sketch from Nature by Asher B. Durand

Letters on Landscape Painting
Letter VII

Dear Sir,

We have seen that of the three primary colors, two are warm and one cold. Whatever connection may be traced between this fact and the attractiveness of their respective qualities, it appears that the general predilection is in favor of the warm in a direct ratio, and justly so, yet I am persuaded that the prevailing fondness for warm color is often indulged to a morbid degree, and the artist too often disposed to gratify it at the expense of truth.

This is especially the case in pictures representing summer (except in sunsets), the prevailing hue at that season being cool, and there is wisdom in the provision – the sensation of coolness conveyed through the eye seems to allay the fervor of the feeling, and render the heat more endurable, so that it would appear a sacrilege to pollute its freshness by an undue proportion of warm color.

I hope that what has already been said in relation to the effect of sunshine and atmosphere, in connection with greenness of color, is sufficient to show that there are effectual means for avoiding all unpleasant coldness, as well as monotony, without sacrificing the sentiment that belongs to, and is inseparable from, the freshness of summer verdure. Green, it is true, is a cool color, but in sunshine it becomes warm green, by a marked addition of yellow. If this be still cool in comparison with other warm colors, it is not cold nor chilly, but of an agreeable temperature, between the two extremes. I have said that light develops color, so the weaker the light the less apparent the color; at the same time the brightest light is most destructive of all color, as seen in its climax on rounded or curvilinear surfaces – on glossy or shining objects becoming white. The true color, then, is in the medium or great mass of light, and the just negation of this highlight or climax, and the gradual transition of the great mass into the shadow, conduce more than all else to the prevention of what is understood by the term paintiness.

Truth of color and general harmony, whether of warmth or coolness, will satisfy every eye; if the picture fail in these it is false somewhere, and if the artist devotes himself with overweening fondness to a preconceived notion of any particular *quality* of color, without a primary regard to truth in its adaptation to his subject, be can scarcely fail to produce an incongruity, and fix the attention of the observer on the nice mixture of pigments rather than on the sentiment of his work. Nothing is more common among pretentious critics, as well as artists, than commendations of this and that picture for certain *fine qualities* of color; it is a favorite theme with the conventionalist, and when these peculiar qualities evince extraordinary skill, all other considerations are thrown aside, and the painter becomes distinguished for that alone. Thus many a young artist is sadly misled to seek for something that he does not see nor feel, and blindly fall into servile imitation of some prominent leader in the display of these much lauded qualities.

Among the most attractive of these peculiarities, perhaps, some of the various shades of grey will be found most prominent. This is likely to be the case from its real importance and value as found in Nature. In some degree grey is almost always present; at times so delicately seen as scarcely to be perceptible, at others more visible, yet liable to be overlooked unless sought for, and at all times so quiet and unobtrusive, it seems to admonish the artist that if he would secure the benefit of its presence, he must never give it undue prominence – it is the summer breeze that chastens the heat of all warm colors, and tempers the cold ones into an harmonious union with them; it is accordingly a department of specific color that well deserves our attention.

Simple grey is perfectly neutral; it becomes warm or cool as it inclines to either of those departments. But we will, for present convenience, divide it into two others, viz. local and circumstantial. It is local when it constitutes the actual color of objects, as in rocks and trunks of trees, and circumstantial when produced by atmosphere and light, as in the shadows of receding objects. It is indeed the principal ingredient in atmospheric tone. The great difficulty in its management (being the most subtle of all tints), is felt in this and other cases of its circumstantial application, as will appear.

Its great value, and the principal test of its admirable quality, consists, first, in its adaptation, that is, to modify the local color of objects according to distance, without supplanting it; or, in other words, to represent local color under the influence of atmosphere; and it insinuates itself thus among all other colors, not only in the broad expanse of distance, but throughout every successive plane up to the foreground of the picture, in foliage, earth and water, being the basis of that beautiful neutrality which conceals or discloses the positive character of all colors, without impairing their beauty.

Its judicious management, therefore, more than all else, perhaps, distinguishes the fine landscape colorist, being neither more nor less than strict conformity to the process, by which Nature reveals and sets off to the greatest advantage her more positive and attractive brilliancy. Not that the tone of his picture is felt to be grey – on the contrary, he so conceals its specific quality, that we only receive the impression of local or natural color. For instance, when the forest texture of the mountain is caused to maintain its native verdure, in spite of the grey veil with which distance has enveloped it, we feel it to be green, but do not see it so, and the same with other objects and colors in like circumstances.

When any palpable form of grey pervades the picture, by usurping the rights of other colors, and staring at you as positive personal grey, instead of being confined to its natural localities or circumstantial functions, its assumption renders it not only objectionable, but next to worthless.

I have particularized the grey tint, as being, from its frequent abuse, one of the by-paths that may embarrass your progress; but I would equally caution you against the allurements of any other peculiar technicality, which may divert your attention from the general aim and meaning of the picture.

All the best artists have shown that the greatest achievement in the producing of fine color, is the concealment of pigments, and not the parade of them; and we may say the same of execution. The less apparent the means and manner of the artist, the more directly will his work appeal to the understanding and the feelings. I shall never forget the reply of Allston to some friends who were praising a very young student in Art for great cleverness, especially in the *freedom* of his execution. "Ah," said he, "that is what we are trying all our lives to get rid of." With that he opened a closet, and brought out a study of a head that he had painted from life, when a young man, at one sitting, and placed it beside a finished work on his easel, at which we had been looking. "There," said he, "that is freely painted." No other comment was required; in the one, paint and the brush attracted attention, in the other, neither was visible, nothing but the glow of light and color which told its truth to Nature – and thus it is with the works of all the greatest colorists. Their skill is perceived in the concealment of the means by which the desired effect is attained, consequently their productions defy the utmost sagacity of the critical examiner to detect any specific mixture or compound by which their characteristic excellence has been attained. It is neither warmth nor coolness that elicits admiration; force nor delicacy; high key nor low key; but always harmony and entire subordination of means. Now, we are not to suppose that this subordination has been especially aimed at by the artist, but that it is the consequence of the process by which higher aims have been reached.

Execution is simply the mode of applying paint to the canvas. It is praiseworthy when it gives assurance of correctness in drawing, and of the knowledge and feeling that have guided the hand. By far too much importance is often attached to it, and the young artist is apt to regard it as one of the first objects of his pursuit, instead of the natural consequence of his practice. Your execution will be good in proportion to your knowledge and skill in drawing; when it becomes conspicuous as a principal feature of the picture, it is presumptive evidence, at least, of deficiency in some higher qualities. So, your coloring will more likely be good, or even excellent, when it does not arrest the attention by any strong peculiarity, and thus divert the eye and mind from the superior considerations of design, composition and character.

I have maintained throughout these letters, the distinction between the mere pleasing picture and that of the true representation of Nature. And I am aware that there is, and always has been, a certain class of critics and commentators on Art, who deny the fact, or contend that something more is required to constitute high Art. What that something is, remains unsettled: but so far as I have had occasion to examine the celebrated works in which such critics have supposed this something to exist, I have never been able to discern its presence, unless the studied artificiality or imbecile attempts to supply imaginary deficiencies in the pictorial imagery of Nature be so construed. If such be the point at issue, we have yet to discover a single instance wherein Art has gained anything by the subterfuge, or the artist not lost by his egotism and vain glory. All that has made Claude preeminent, is truthfulness of representation in his light and atmosphere, and moving waters – if other portions of his works were equally *true*, he would be still greater. And why have the nobler compositions of Gaspar Poussin only given him an inferior rank, but because they lack in corresponding truthfulness. I might instance hundreds of others, ancient and modern, who owe their reputation to the degree of representative and imitative truth which distinguishes their works. Closing the list with the name of Turner, who has gathered from the previously unexplored sky alone, transcripts of Nature, whose mingled beauty of form and chiaroscuro have immortalized him, for the sole reason that he has therein approached nearer to the representation of the infinity of Nature than all that have gone before him.

I do not say that simple naturalness necessarily makes a picture great, but that none can be great without it; for Nature herself is unequal, in the eye of Art. It is the province of Art, then, and all the license that the artist can claim or desire, is to choose the time and place where she displays her chief perfections, whether of beauty or majesty, repose or action. Let her sittings be thus controlled, and the artist will have no occasion to idealize the portrait, no need to shape her features on his classic model – or eke out an expression that he does not see – no need to modify the light and shade that develop the fullness of her graceful form and matchless color; and every accessory from the vast folding of her cloud-curtain to the embroidered footstool beneath, will be furnished of such cast and fitness, as to require no change at his hands. There is not a tint of color, nor phase of light and dark, force or delicacy, gradation or contrast, or any charm that the most inventive imagination ever employed or conceived worthy to be regarded as beautiful or for any other quality, fitting to the aim of Art, that is not to be seen in Nature, more beautiful and more fitting than Art has ever realized or ever can; and there is no acknowledged excellence in any picture extant, which justly commands our admiration, which has not been transcribed, more or less faithfully, from her glorious volume.

Then, why should we resort to pictures, or the study of Art, independent of, or embracing any other mode than that which has direct reference to the original source whence Art has sprung? For no other purpose surely than to aid, perchance, the growth of our perceptions, and advance our knowledge of the province and capacity of Art. In this respect much may be gained to the saving of time and labor, but it has its evils and its dangers – if indiscriminately relied on, it may do more harm than good.

If the absence of naturalness, or what we term truth, could be compensated for by any other artistic excellence, even that of the most brilliant imaginative power, we might commend the student to the study of pictures, instead of Nature, to a greater extent even than is now in vogue, for he will find in the works of great masters all that could be desired of executive and constructive merit, and occasionally, perhaps, examples of as great a degree of representative and imitative truth as Art can ever attain, and with adequate perception and enlightened judgment to discern and appreciate these qualities, he may, indeed, profit by the study; but without experimental knowledge of, and overruling reliance on, the great principles which he perceives and feels as existing in Nature, and keeping them constantly present in his mind, such study will be of little avail, and may be detrimental. For it is the manner or style of the picture, unfortunately, which first engages the attention of the inexperienced student; and, as every true artist has his *own* manner, i.e., certain peculiarities of execution, etc., the result of his organization, a picture is not available as a subject for study, with the view to the formation of your style, or for any other practical benefit. It is not the manner that you are to study, but to confine your examination of pictures to the discovery of the less obvious means employed, and the capacity of the materials of Art toward the representation of Nature, especially in all that indicates the treatment or disposition of the respective parts, so as to give the greatest prominence to the most essential characteristics.

Pictures abound which display the complete mastery of all the technicalities of Art, fascinating by the most dexterous execution and brilliancy of color, yet false to Nature and destitute of all that awakens thought or interests the feelings; yet they attract the eye, satisfy the superficial observer, and deceive the unguarded Art student, especially when sustained by the loud commendations of the spurious critic, who, rejecting the standard of Nature, erects in its place his unmeaning ideal, and fancies he finds it realized in every skillful novelty which artistic egotism displays. This is a condition incidental to, and inseparable from, the very Nature of Art, and only removable by the force of that discriminating perception which the study of Nature alone can impart.

Yours, truly,
A. B. Durand

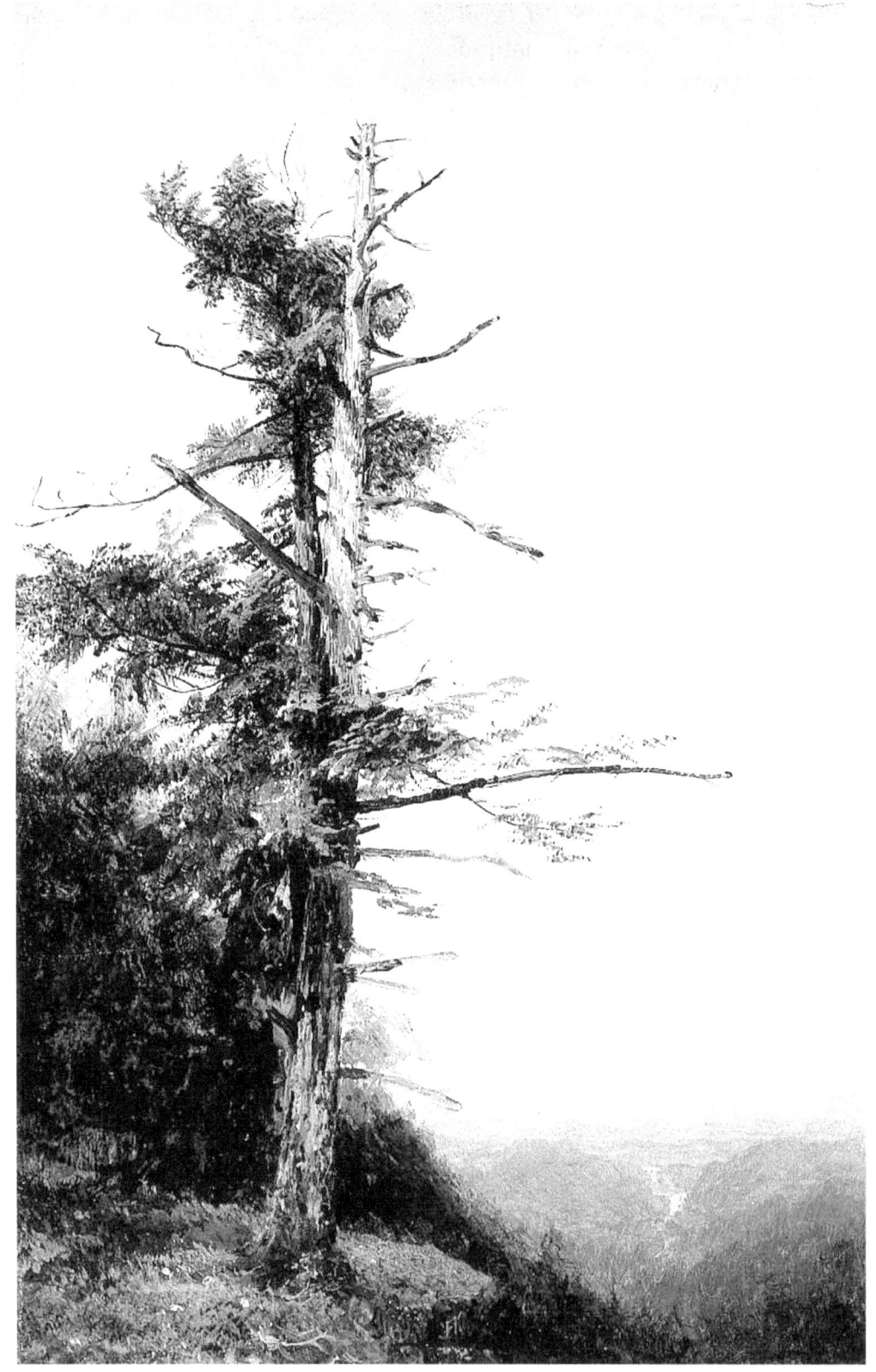

The Hemlock by John F. Kensett, 1870

Studying from Nature

Editor's note:
The following article appeared in the June 6, 1855 issue of *The Crayon,* just before Durand's eighth letter. Its author is unknown but was likely Durand's son, John.

As the season for sketching is about commencing, it would seem to be in place that we should make some suggestions to our younger artists, and to amateurs who will determinedly set about the Study of Nature, that may facilitate the labor of making studies of landscape. These hints will be drawn not only from personal experience, but from a knowledge of the methods of distinguished landscape painters, obtained by personal acquaintance in most cases. It must, however, be remembered, that method is, after all, only an expression of an artist's peculiar way of regarding Nature, and that the method which is very useful to one may be unavailable to an artist of different mental constitution, and no method that we could prescribe would meet entirely the wants of any one, though there may be valuable suggestions given. We are not believers to any extent in the efficacy of manner – we think that the most important thing is to find *what to paint* – the *how to paint it* will come in due time.

It is necessary to understand, firstly, that the great object to be gained in studying from Nature, is the strengthening of the memory, for the artist who carries away from the scene he has sketched no more than is on his paper or canvas, can, when he reaches his studio, do nothing but reproduce his sketch, a most tame and profitless exercise. He must store his memory with facts and impressions, which his sketches shall recall at his pleasure – and the more tenacious and comprehensive his memory, the more powerful as a painter of landscape will he be.

In this exercise of the memory two things are to be kept in sight, viz., – that a full and entire knowledge of any object is necessary to enable us to recall it clearly, and that to strengthen the memory, it is necessary to task it constantly.* The first thing, then, to be done by the student, is to learn thoroughly the facts which any object presents to his vision; and, in order to do this, it is well to make the most faithful studies possible, even to daguerreotype minuteness, although it should not be desirable to paint pictures with the same minuteness; because, the more exact one's knowledge of the details and his recollection of them, the fuller will be his conceptions, not only of the parts, but of the whole. In making studies from Nature, therefore, it is not possible to finish too highly, and, indeed, no young artist ought ever to make sketches, properly so called, which are rather the memoranda to be used by those whose knowledge and memory are full, and who need only a hint to bring out their ideas. Beginners should do nothing slightly, but should rather finish a very few things perfectly, than to do any number with half completeness. A single study made in this spirit will bring more improvement than ten times the amount of labor less earnestly bestowed. And remember that finish does not consist in glossy manipulation, but in the fullness of rendering of the minutiae. It does not matter what you work with, whether with pencil, in oils, or in watercolor; *tell the facts*, however awkwardly; you can leave out or modify as you please afterward, you may forget unpleasant things, as you generally will – but learn everything to begin with. Do not let the smallest marking in the bark of a tree, the most delicate shadow in the distance, escape you; you cannot tell how important memory or your imagination may make them.

Supposing the student to be well acquainted with the principles of drawing, and to have sufficient facility in that direction to need no instructions there, the most useful method would be to commence in oil color as the easiest of management, and selecting some very simple piece of foreground material, to make his trial in the full determination to be satisfied with the study before he leaves it. More than he can well imagine depends on his success or failure in this first trial. Triumph will inspirit him, and lead to fuller successes, while the abandonment of the effort with a sense of defeat, will produce a permanent weakness. It is even advantageous to commence at one part of the study, usually at the top, and finish every minutest object before leaving it – and thus the most trivial thing realized, gives something inspiriting to look back to. We believe that many an artist has been injured irretrievably by having relinquished his first effort, before he was satisfied (or approximately so) with it; it has been like a child's first falsehood. Oil color, by the facilities it gives for over-working, renders the success more certain, and so far is to be preferred; but, we imagine that the ultimate result is much the same, whatever material or method may be used. J. B. Pyne, the eminent English landscape painter, recommends the student to make first by an elaborate pencil drawing of the subject in outline, without any regard to the character of the drawing, or to light and shade; then, making a reduction of the drawing, to wash in with watercolor, the effect as seen in Nature, and the general color without regard to detail. The majority of the English landscapists who paint in oil, however, make careful studies in the same material – and, indeed, in many cases paint their pictures, if of small size, entirely on the spot, as Creswick, who paints with great facility, and mere transcripts of Nature. Our own Cole painted, we believe, from pencil outlines simply; but this is a dangerous course for a young artist, as he neglects to study tone and the subtler relations of light and shade, and in time loses his sense of color, unless he have a very strong feeling for it. Durand makes his studies entirely in oil, finishing carefully, but generally of parts only.

But however you choose to work, you will find your facility increase according to your earnestness. The systematic training of the memory is a thing rarely attempted, and yet perfectly easy, and of so great use, that some artists have insisted that the true method of study was to go out and look at Nature, then, returning from her, to paint from recollection. By doing this repeatedly, each time correcting some error, or supplying some deficiency, the improvement in the memory will be astonishing. But, there are many to whom this is impossible; and there are very few, indeed, capable of retaining nice distinctions of form for even a short time, and the tendency of this system would be to make the student lose sight of detail to a great extent – but as an auxiliary to the faithful study before Nature, it must be of great use. Look at a marked tree trunk, for instance, and, after making all the mental observations on it you please, go home and attempt to draw it, and you will probably find that you know nothing of its form – or if you recollect certain traits, you will find most assuredly when you come to compare the drawing with the original, that you recalled it very imperfectly; yet each time that you pass from Nature to the drawing, the image will grow more distinct. For the reproduction of transitory effects in landscape, particularly, this exercise is invaluable, as the fullest aid from sketches is necessarily very slight.

But this one thing ever remember, that before Nature you are to lose sight of yourself, and seek reverently for truth, neither being captious as to what its quality may be, or considering whether your manner of telling it may be the most dexterous and draughtsmanlike. It is not of the least consequence whether *you* appear in your studies or no – it is of the highest importance that they should be true. You will find, in after times, that the rudest effort to tell a fact in Nature will have a value, which will shame your studied prettinesses into the obscurity of rubbish portfolios.

*For more information about training one's visual memory, see *Memory Drawing: Perceptual Training and Recall*, by Darren R. Rousar.

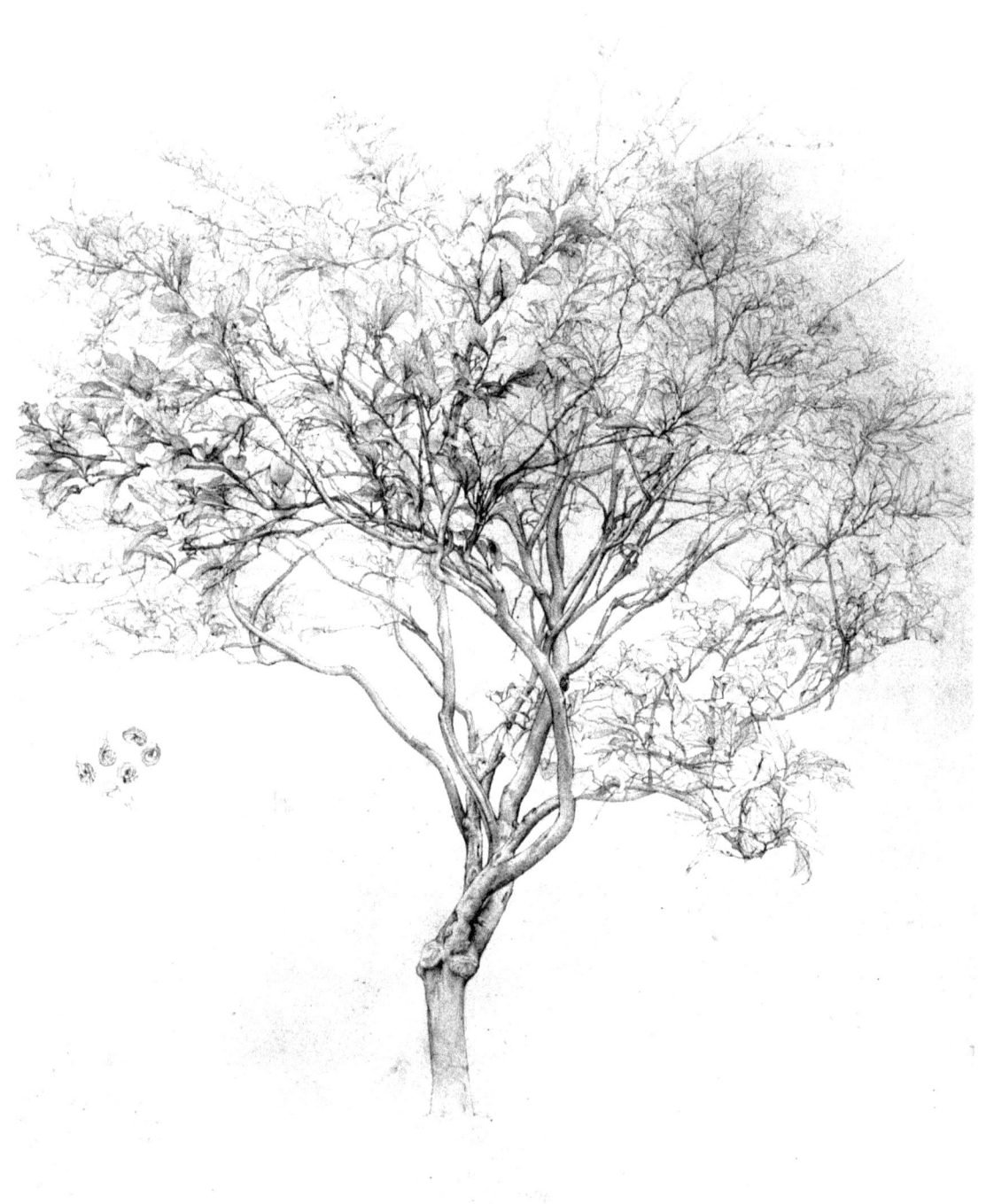

Study of a Lemon Tree by Frederick Leighton

Letters on Landscape Painting
Letter VIII

Dear Sir,

A Landscape with figures, introduced merely for pictorial effect, without enhancing the meaning, may render the picture more beautiful and more artistic, and yet amount to little more than a sort of human cattle-piece; and whenever the human figure becomes paramount, and gives to the picture a significance independent of, and superseding the sentiment of the landscape, it is no longer legitimate landscape, and falls under some of the departments of figure subjects. But when the human form exerts an influence in unison, with the sentiment of inanimate nature, increasing its significance without supplanting it, the representative character of the landscape is not affected; and whatever imaginative force may attach to the figure itself, the value of representative truth is not lessened. When I asserted, then, in my last letter, that the great landscape is always representative of, nature, and that it owes its greatness primarily to this fact, it was on the ground previously assumed, that the true province of Landscape Art is the representation of the work of God in the visible creation, independent of man or not dependent on human action, further than as an accessory or an auxiliary. From this point of view let us briefly examine the conventional distinctions of Idealism and Realism, together with the action of the imagination in connection with them, and which seems to have given rise to these distinctions.

What then is Idealism? According to the interpretation commonly received, that picture is ideal whose component parts are representative of the utmost perfection of Nature, whether with respect to beauty or other considerations of fitness in the objects represented, according to their respective kinds, and also the most perfect arrangement or composition of these parts so as to form an equally perfect whole. The extreme of this ideal asserts that this required perfection is not to be found or rarely found in single examples of natural objects, nor in any existing combination of them. In order to compose the ideal picture, then, the artist must know what constitutes the perfection of every object employed, according to its kind, and its circumstances, so as to be able to gather from individuals the collective idea. This view of Idealism does not propose any deviation from the truth, but on the contrary, demands the most rigid adherence to the law of its highest development.

Realism, therefore, if any way distinguishable from Idealism, must consist in the acceptance of ordinary forms and combinations as found. If strictly confined to this, it is, indeed, an inferior grade of Art; but as no one contends that the representation of ordinary or commonplace nature is an ultimatum in Art, the term Realism signifies little else than a disciplinary stage of Idealism, according to the interpretation given, and is misapplied when used in opposition to it, for the ideal is, in fact, nothing more than the perfection of the real.

Every step of progress towards truthful representation of Nature will be so much gained of the knowledge indispensable to the attainment of the ideal, for all the generic elements of natural objects, by which one kind is distinguished from another, are the same in the imperfect as in the perfect specimen. The difference lies in the disposition of them; so when you shall have learned all that characterizes the oak as oak, you will be prepared to apply those characteristics according to the requirements of ideal beauty, to the production of the ideal oak. And this process continued through all forms and combinations, defines the creative power of Art, not in producing new things for its special purpose, but in supplying from Nature's general fullness, all particular deficiencies in whatsoever things she has furnished for its use. Thus far the meaning of Idealism is limited to the perfection of beauty with generic character and fitness in combinations. But the ideal of Landscape Art does not end here; it embraces, and with even higher meaning, the application of these perfections to the expression of a particular sentiment in the subject of the picture – whether it be the representation of the repose and serenity of Nature in quiet and familiar scenes, or of her sterner majesty in the un-trodden wilderness, as well as of her passional action in the whirlwind and storm – each has its own distinctive ideality. In this direction we come to the action of the imaginative faculty, which perfects the high Ideal.

In so far as we have arrived at any understanding of the term Idealism and Realism, there does not appear any definite line of distinction between them, or at best, these terms are inexpressive, if intended to describe separate departments of Art power; nor can I discern wherein the imaginative faculty exercises an influence independent of the perfect ideal of representative truth, but only in extending its meaning to the utmost limit, spiritualizing, as it were, the images of inanimate objects, and appealing through them to the inmost susceptibility of the mind and heart, thus becoming the highest attribute of the great Artist in developing the true ideal. Hence its legitimate action is not seen as creating an imaginary world, as some suppose; but in revealing the deep meaning of the real creation around and within us.

The imagination, like every other element of genius, can only be comprehended in its visible impress on whatsoever things it touches, always identical, but with comparative degrees of power, at times dimly shadowed, at others glowing with impassioned feeling. The faint blush of morning light that calls up the sleeping mists of the valley, may declare its presence as surely as the lurid flash that

"sets on fire.
The heavens with falling thunderbolts."

It is not my purpose, however, to discuss the nature of the imaginative faculty, nor the subtle abstractions of idealism. It is sufficient if we have arrived safely at the conclusion, that all the elements with which the imagination deals, and on which idealism is based, exist visibly in Nature, and are, therefore, not separate creations of Art, my chief object being to guard against the false notion that High Landscape Art disregards all restrictions imposed by the law of truthful representation of nature.

One important inference, at least, is derived from what has been said – that is, if a student who is capable of perceiving and appreciating the beautiful, seldom finds in any given subject selected for study that completeness of individual parts or general arrangement which gives entire satisfaction, and takes on himself the responsibility of changing or omitting objectionable features, with the view to idealize without reference to the principle of ideal beauty, which preserves all characteristic forms inviolate, the chance is, that what is gained in grace will not compensate for the loss of the vigorous expression which it displaces, and that it is better to accept the model as nature has disposed it, without thought of change, until such time as increase of knowledge and mature judgment shall enable him to supply deficiencies without loss of character: for example, to prune the tree, if required, or add an additional branch, as by natural growth, instead of engrafting on it for the sake of beauty in form, offshoots that falsify its particular species.

And further: with motives similar to those which induce the student prematurely to attempt improvements in the model before him, he is often mistakenly impelled to make long journeys in search of the picturesque, in order to gain attention, and win applause, when, by the common roadside, and on the banks of familiar streams near home, provident Nature has furnished elements of ideal beauty easily approached, and more than sufficient for the wants of all the incipient stages of study, and when faithfully transcribed, more essentially beautiful, and more certain to win admiration from those whose approbation is desirable, than any abortive display of the grand and striking features of Nature can ever produce. Extensive scenes of wild or other impressive character, as well as rare and extraordinary effects, are not subjects for the young artist, and why should he seek them when the simple and familiar passages above indicated, like the domestic virtues – not only estimable for their intrinsic loveliness but also for the total absence of ostentation, – and being appreciable by all, will be more certain of just and ample reward.

Much has been said by writers on Art as well as artists, in disparagement of what they call *servile imitation* of Nature, as unworthy of genius and degrading to Art, cramping invention, and fettering the imagination, in short, productive only of mere matter-of-fact works. What is meant by servile imitation, so called, is difficult to understand. If its meaning is limited to that view of realism which accepts commonplace forms and appearances, without searching for the ideal of natural beauty, the objections are valid; but if it comprehends the faithful representation of all that is most beautiful and best fitted for the entire purposes of Art, really existing and accessible, and ever waiting to be gathered up by earnest love and untiring labor, then it is an utter fallacy, born of indolence and conceit. With the faculty to perceive and select from the infinite beauty and significance of Nature broadcast throughout her wide domain, surely no artist can reasonably complain for lack of unbounded liberty. Let him take the pains to store his memory with the unlimited *material* thus furnished, and the inventive and imaginative faculties will have enough to do in developing every conceivable result, and in ample measure for the supply of the most insatiate desires of Art.

It appears to me sheer folly to talk about too close imitation of Nature, in any object or appearance eligible and worthy for the highest or humblest purposes of Art, or of too servile reliance on the continuous practical study of them. Nor can we dispense with such study, unless something more worthy can be found to supply its place, and render the study unnecessary. This, the free-thinking Art-advocate, does not pretend to furnish, but merely demands permission to deviate at pleasure from, or not to be tied down to, literal transcripts. If such transcripts were practicable, which is not the case, the injurious effect of the alleged servility is after all dependent on the capacity of the student, for where the faculties exist to make a right use of all study of Nature, there can be no possible danger, no restriction to the freest exercise; on the other hand, where they do not exist, the fetter, if any be found, will be well applied, and fortunate for Art, if applied to arrest the multiplication of inane compositions and unmeaning details which make up the great majority of landscape pictures everywhere abounding. The supposed evil, then, of this *servile imitation*, is a mere bugbear, and so far as it concerns the unimaginative artist, such a course is his surest safeguard against the repetition and sameness, of whatsoever description, to which he is constantly exposed.

Who has ever seen the glowing sunlight or transparent silvery atmosphere too servilely imitated? The playful surface or thoughtful depth of lucid waters – their rage when swollen by the outpourings of heaven, or lashed into foam by the mighty winds – who has imitated these too servilely? And the like beauty and sublimity of the glorious sky – when shall we see an imitation too servile of its eternal changefulness? The long processions of the quiet cirri, in their robes of purity skirting the gorgeous thrones of majestic cumuli, and the dark rain-clouds, agitated and convulsed with awful threatenings, like a revolutionary tumult,

> "– with fear of change
> Perplexing monarchs!"

And then, before the agile hand can have traced some record of their brief existence, fading away in filmy light, or losing form in broad mysterious shadows, and again reviving in different forms and combinations, now dim with foreboding gloom, now rivaling the sun in dazzling splendor, with every intermediate gradation and contrast within the range of human perception can this be imitated at all, much less too servilely!

And in many other constituents of the great picture – according to their purport and consequence – the most beautiful tree of its species – the rock, for its picturesqueness with generic character – wherein is there danger on the score of truthful servility? And finally, why is every distinguished Landscapist noted for constant outdoor studiousness, – Claude, according to Vasari, from morning till nightfall at work in the open fields or on the quays, from whence he drew his far-famed sea-ports – Turner, at all hours under the open sky, *washing in* his memoranda of the flitting effects which display his imaginative power and versatile invention! and other diligent students of Nature of like habits. Why should such men be forever toiling at the great fountain, if the artificial cisterns of the studio were not inadequate to quench their thirst?

Let us away, then, with these false alarms, and be thankful in the assurance that it is by reverent attention to the realized forms of Nature alone, that Art is enabled by its delegated power to reproduce some measure of the profound and elevated emotions which the contemplation of the visible works of God awaken. Could the picture do more by means of whatsoever Art-license or departure from the truth?

Imitation of Nature is indeed servile, and every way unworthy, when it discards the necessity of selection, and indiscriminately accepts all things as of equal value, not only bestowing the same care on the wild thistle of the field as on the rose and on the passion-flower, but without discerning the twofold commendations of superior beauty and significance, as indicated in the perfume and in the symbolism which invest the latter with higher claims to a place in the Art-conservatory.

Yours truly,
A. B. Durand

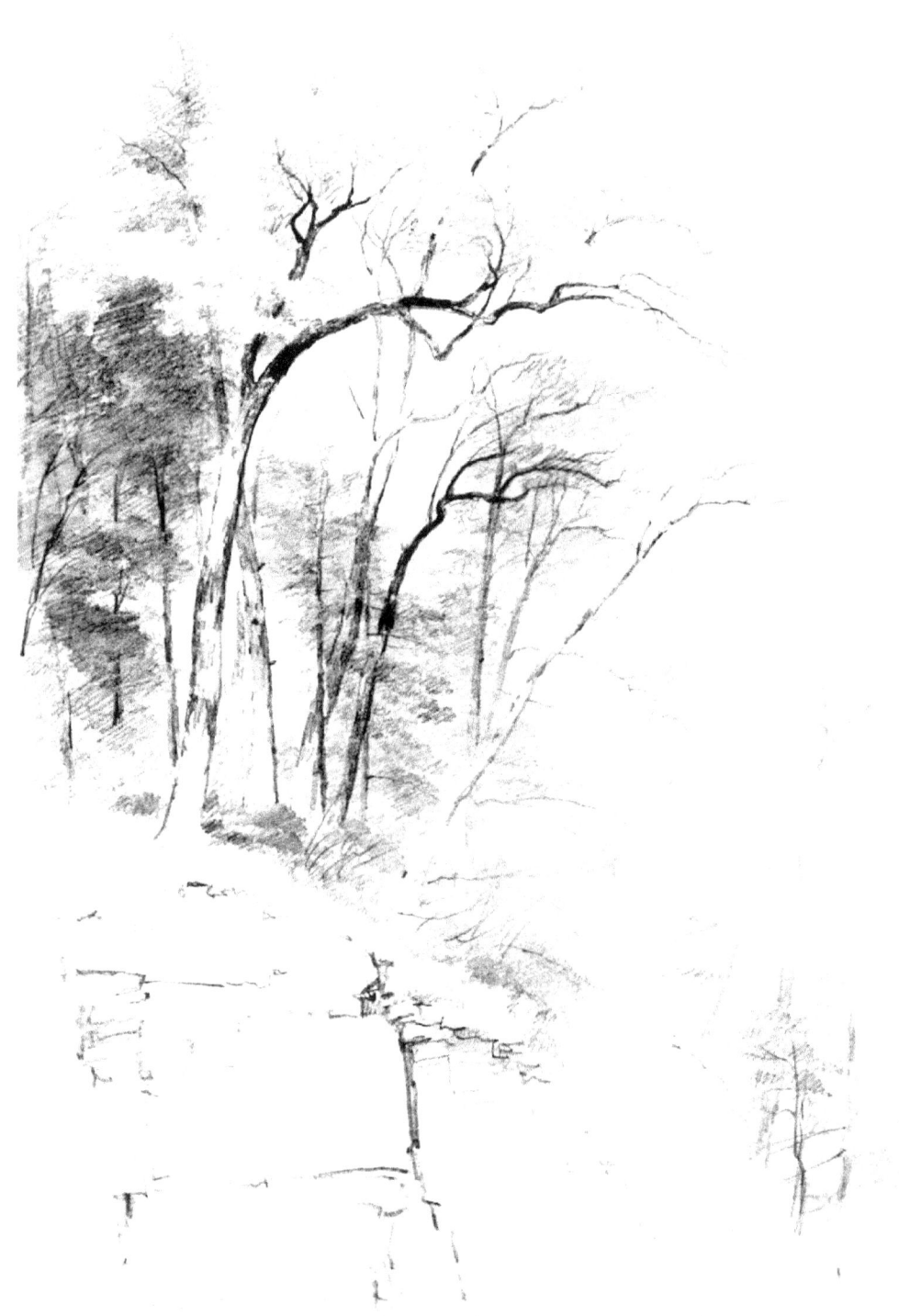

Study of Trees and Rocks, Kaaterskill Clove, New York by Asher B. Durand, 1850

Letters on Landscape Painting
Letter IX

Dear Sir,

If you have ever ascended a high mountain, even by a well-defined path, you must have encountered many difficulties, in crag and chasm, and other unforeseen obstacles, and have, at least, practically learned, that a short sentence of directions involved miles of toilsome labor, and it is thus with the precepts and practice of Art; especially in the direction I have endeavored to point out. But believing it to be the direct path to the main summit, I could not commend an easier way to a secondary elevation. As far as my experience and observation extend, I have uniformly found that coldness and opacity of color, stiffness and hardness of contour, with a general repulsiveness in effect, characterize, for the most part, the early efforts of the conscientious student of Nature. He often becomes disheartened, and almost persuaded, on comparing his own with the productions of the mature artist, that the beauty of the latter is the result of deviation from, rather than adherence to the truth. In such an inference he may be greatly mistaken, as will appear, on close examination, and instead of being regarded as discouraging, it should be construed in the opposite direction. In the first place, much practice and observation are indispensable to the acquirement of the mechanical skill necessary to express the precision with the *delicacy* of Nature's outlines; so that the first endeavors will invariably result in hardness, if not ungracefulness, just in proportion to the conscientiousness of the effort; and then, if the student be peculiarly sensitive to the attraction of form, color is sure to be overlooked, and even so far as observed, his representation of it will more likely be too cold than otherwise, for the great mass of local color, out of sunlight, is, at least, neutral, inclining to coolness, and even the additional warmth imparted by sunlight is attributable to its glow as much as to its actual warmth in color. And this glow, be it remembered, is the great charm and secret of light, most difficult to realize.

Now, I have already stated that imitation, if ever desirable, is unattainable except to a very limited extent, and above all, most limited in reference to the glow of sunlight. If, then, we attempt to express it by matching its local color, the inherent lack of the glowing quality in our pigments, defeats the aim, and as warmth is the local distinctive quality of the light, we find, by increasing its apparent warmth, a nearer approach to the glowing is attained. This may be called one of the licenses of Art, or rather one of its modes for attaining a more perfect representation of that which is inimitable in Nature. As a general rule, then, we must express the real by increasing the apparent warmth of light, or, at least, keep on the warm side rather than the cold. And, further, in regard to hardness of outline; the forms of objects – the lines of separation or relief from each other – are easily misconceived, or not truly estimated by the eye. We perceive objects in juxtaposition to be decidedly detached from each other, and so they are, but rarely by any uniform line of separation, either dark or light, though occasionally sharp and cutting in these respects; but more frequently they are blended or assimilated with each other, so that the real cause of separation is found in a few points of sharp light or dark, aided as may be by color. The principle of relief or separation of parts is one of the most subtle and capricious in Nature, and accordingly, most likely to perplex the young student, since it never ceases to be a puzzle to the practiced artist. If we cannot follow all the modes by which Nature carries out this principle, we must adopt such as are found to be most sure and practicable, and, at the same time, most beautiful. Among them is that of *variety*, that is, unequal hardness and softness, of contour, contrast of color, and abruptness and gradation in light and dark; for example, any prominent object uniformly relieved by the same strength of outline, however beautiful in itself, may thereby become offensive, yet Nature often thus presents herself: on the other hand, she as often varies that relief as above stated, and we feel its superior beauty. The trunk of a tall tree, or a long line of horizon, objectionable because of their monotony, become agreeable by inequality of relief, losing their contour in one place, and sharply defining it in another. This may suffice for the present to indicate somewhat of the process by which Art transcribes Nature, not only selecting her most beautiful and expressive forms, but choosing with equal care among the various influences by which they are affected in relation to each other, and it may be also taken as a hint in reference to what are termed licenses of Art.

If you find, that in order to obtain the glow of light, you must increase its warmth of color, you are licensed to do it; if continued sharpness of outline is offensive, you are licensed to vary it, because Nature herself is variable on these points, and because one condition is more beautiful than the other. But when it is simply a question of choice, there is no license, *that* signifying the liberty to deviate from law, and since Art is inadequate to represent *all* Nature's beauty with equal truthfulness, there is no law to interfere with whatsoever license that shall be found to increase its representative power. The extent of such license must forever remain a disputable question. But I believe that none are desirable which oppose any of the great truths of Nature, and that it is rather permission to exaggerate certain points in order to represent their real importance, as by increasing the warmth of light to express its glow, or to give more than natural intensity to a dark, in order to express the force of surrounding light, and, if needs be, to keep subordinate objects from impertinent obtrusiveness, by subduing their natural attractiveness, whether of details, color, or magnitude. To express the apparent height of a mountain, it is found necessary to exaggerate the real elevation in the representation: this is a license not opposed to truth, but essential to its realization. Whatever, then, may be the extent of Art-license, one thing is certain, it can never be profitably exercised but for the more complete expression of the sentiment of Nature, material and spiritual, wherein we discern the true mission of Art.

Perhaps we may pursue the subject of license still further to advantage. In requiring adherence to truthful representation, I wish not, to be understood as insisting on literal portraiture, even in cases of actual view painting, that is, with regard to the entire details of any given scene. There can be no scene worthy of being painted, that does not possess certain characteristic features, which constitute its interest. These features are obvious at a glance, and must be preserved inviolate; there are others more or less subordinate, – such should receive attention according to their relative importance; and there are still others of no importance at all, and may be disposed of at the pleasure of the artist, so long as they are not rendered obtrusive. Now, the artist is not only licensed, but enjoined to modify, or entirely omit all these subordinate details, whenever they detract from the beauty, or other interest of predominant features; when he has acquired the knowledge necessary to do it with certainty. He may displace a tree, for instance, if disagreeable, or render it a more perfect one of its kind if retained, but the elevations and depressions of the earth's surface composing the middle ground and distance, the magnitude of objects, and extent of space presented in the view, characteristic outline, undulating or angular, of all the great divisions, may not be changed in the least perceptible degree, most especially the mountain and hill forms. On these God has set his signet, and Art may not remove it when the picture professes to represent the scene. Nor is it to be desired; for the ever-changing sky sends down the winged messengers of cloud and sunshine that overrule the refractory contours, unfolding to the utmost the beauty of the beautiful, and veiling with discriminating care the unlovely portions.

View painting is ranked as the inferior department of landscape Art, and, generally speaking, it is so, inasmuch as it precludes the exercise of the creative power in invention and composition. But it does not preclude the action of the imagination in all that relates to effect and color, and although it is not permitted to violate the integrity of portraiture, it may invest its portraits with the same profound expression that the imagination impresses on the ideal picture. And while it affords the only safe ground for the unimaginative, it is one of the most signal achievements of the imaginative artist, in demonstration of his superiority. For his loftier stature enables him to overlook, without trespass, the enclosure which bounds the view of humbler minds – he comprehends the capabilities of the material presented in all its relations to human sympathy (whether already combined in the actual view, or noted on the tablet of memory), and he reads the historic record which time has written on all things for our instruction, through all the stages of their silent transition, since the period when this verdant earth was a lifeless, molten chaos, "void and without form."

However subordinate the department of view-painting may be considered in its general sense, it rises at times to the level of the highest creations of Art, so far as the *expression* of its elements is concerned. Many an actual picture of this description may be found amongst the primitive wilds of Nature, where

"Upon her bosom yet
After the lapse of untold centuries,
The freshness of her far-beginning lies."

The reverent imagination ceases to exult in its own conscious power to change and recreate, while it contemplates the great miracle of God's creation, "which still goes on in silence" – where all deficiency in picturesqueness is more than supplied by that "freshness of the far-beginning" of things which connects us with the past, and symbolizes our immortality.

I would not limit the creative power of Art, nor undervalue its importance; it may not be possible to define or know its limit, but we do know that it is worthily employed, when it reproduces by actual transcript, or otherwise, a sensible demonstration of

"The perpetual work of thy creation,
Finished, yet removed forever,"

and unfolds by the "eloquence of beauty," and signs of "healing sympathy," perpetual sources of enlightened and pure enjoyment.

Yours truly,
A. B. Durand

LANDSCAPE PAINTING

BY
BIRGE HARRISON

EDITED FROM THE
ORIGINAL, 1910 PUBLICATION

NEW YORK
CHARLES SCRIBNER'S SONS
1910

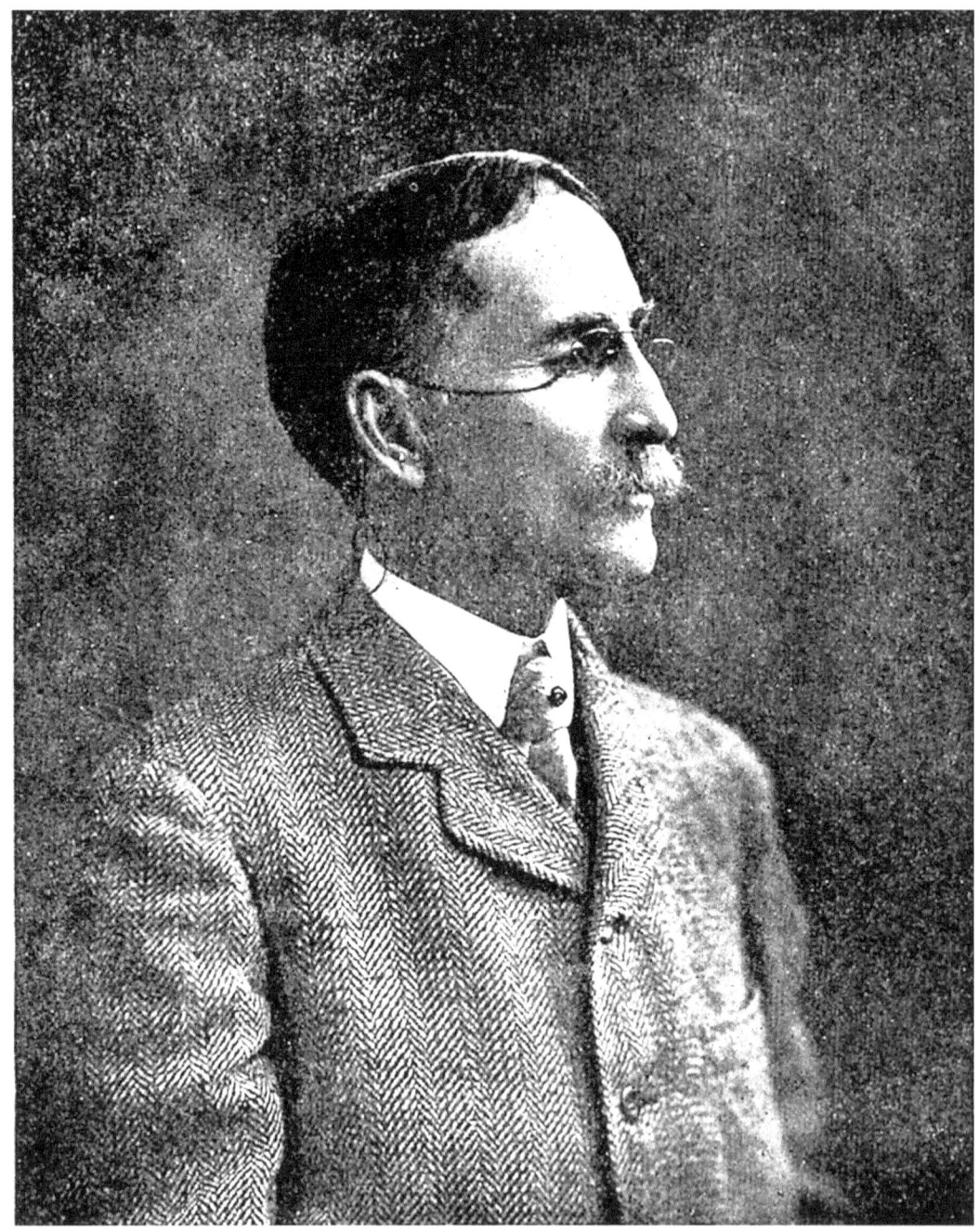

L. Birge Harrison, 1914

ORIGINAL FOREWORD

This little book represents the fulfilment of a promise to put into permanent form certain impromptu talks on landscape painting given before the Art Students' League of New York at its summer school at Woodstock, NY. No effort has been made to elaborate the themes treated, the writer feeling that what might be gained in literary form might very well be lost in spontaneity and conciseness of statement. It is hardly necessary to say that these little talks make no claim to infallibility of judgment. They simply represent the present beliefs and convictions of a painter who is himself still a student; but they are sincere, at least, and "straight from the shoulder."

It is to be regretted that the art of color printing has not yet reached a stage of development where it can be trusted with the reproduction of a masterpiece of landscape, which often depends for its beauty on color-tones and color-transitions of extreme delicacy. In the present volume it has been judged best to confine the reproductions to simple half-tones in black and white –to give no color rather than color which is false and misleading; and the illustrations here included are therefore presented, not as adequate representations of the works themselves, but as hints and suggestions only of the qualities which give to those works their distinction and their beauty.

Thanks are due to the editors of Scribner's Magazine, The North American Review, The International Studio, and Palette and Brush for permission to reprint here certain of the chapters which have already appeared in the publications mentioned.

B. H.
Woodstock, N. Y., 1909.

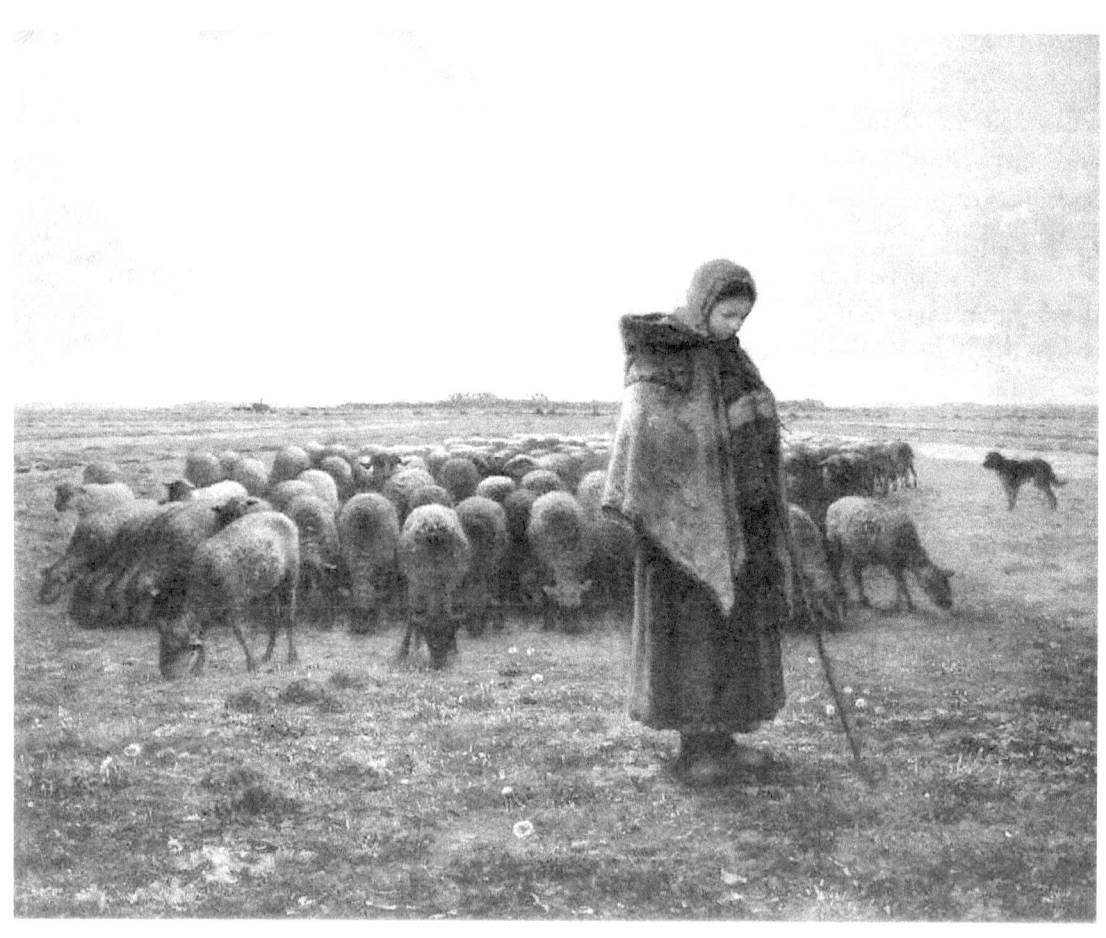

Jean-Francois Millet
Shepherdess with Her Flock

·I·

Landscape Art in General

For some occult reason in which the two factors of race and psychology are intimately blended, landscape art in its best expression is and ever has been confined within the narrow geographical limits of Northern and Western Europe. Oriental art – the art of Persia, Japan, and India – has always been more or less abstract and symbolical; and, as the art of a people invariably reflects the character of the race which gave it birth, we may deduce with certainty the character of the Oriental from the character of his art. By reversing the same reasoning we reach the conclusion that the simple existence of our Aryan ancestors (lived close to nature in the constant companionship of elemental things) has found expression in the landscape art of their remote descendants. The artistic temperament is no growth of a day. It has its roots in the far-away beginnings of a people and we make no unwarranted presumption in asserting that the landscape or marine painter of today is at last giving expression to the groping instincts and ideals of his cave-dwelling forbears. The blinding storms with which they battled, the mountains they scaled in the pursuit of game, the waves they rode in their primitive canoes, the hard winters that froze their blood, and the soft spring suns that warmed them. They were the first to see and to record the pearly tones of outdoor nature, and their technical bequest to posterity was an extended gamut of grays and mauves and lilacs which remain upon the artist's palette to the present day.

A scant half-dozen of their pictures drifted over to France, and there became the inspiration of a new art movement, which finally resulted in the great school of Barbizon. Millet and Troyon, Corot and Rousseau incontestably produced greater work than Crome and Constable, but their pictures were all painted on the lines marked out by the Englishmen. Indeed, it is questionable if we should have ever had a Barbizon school had it not been for the iconoclasts across the Channel.

While the great Barbizon school of painters was still in its prime, there appeared upon the artistic horizon another band of innovators who have since become known as the French Impressionists or Luminarists. They were in reality, as their name implies, painters of light, and their technique was founded upon the scientific principle that light is essentially prismatic. White, being made up of the three primary colors – red, yellow, and blue – should so be painted, they declared, the three pure pigments lying side by side upon the canvas – and the same with red, with yellow, and with blue; there could be no blue so powerful that it would not be qualified with touches of red and yellow, no yellow so brilliant that the red and the blue were not felt in its composition, no red so intense that the blue and the yellow did not play across it. The work of these men really seems to vibrate with light, and the word "vibration," first employed by them, has now been permanently added to the artists' vocabulary. Under the leadership of Pissaro, Sisley, and Monet they delivered a message which future artists can never afford to ignore.

But, while their discovery is sound in principle, no entirely satisfactory technical method of applying it to the painting of pictures has yet been discovered. It is certain that the dots and dashes and cross-hatched strokes of pure color generally used by the Luminarists do not render the effect of nature as seen by the ordinary cultivated eye. The veteran Monet himself has lived long enough to recognize this, and in his more recent work he has abandoned his early militant method, while retaining the general principle of broken color.

This is one of the unsolved problems of art that we moderns have to work out. Another is the question of how best to convey the impression of motion upon the rigidly quiescent surface of a canvas. This has never been accomplished, but to assert that it is impossible would be a hazardous statement. Still another problem derives from the limitations of the human eye. A good photographic lens will see every leaf upon a tree or every individual in a crowd of ten thousand people. The human eye can see at best but a dozen or two of leaves or people, the remainder producing the effect of a more or less indefinite blur. How is this blur to be rendered with just sufficient definition to produce the desired effect upon the spectator? It is quite certain that other problems will arise, problems as unsuspected today as was the prismatic theory of light a hundred years ago. It is impossible of course to particularize. One small discovery frequently leads to a much greater one, and the only thing we can predict with certainty is that the unexpected will occur. But we do at least know that the door is ajar, that the glorious sunlight is out there, just beyond, and that nothing can keep us longer cooped up indoors.

·II·

Color

We are all born color-blind. The most perfect eyes in the world cannot see one quarter of the colors which are known to exist in nature. Those of us who are fortunate, it is true, are able to differentiate with reasonable exactness the three primary colors which go to make up our limited human color-scale – but what about the tones which certainly exist above the ultraviolet band and below the infrared?

For convenience, the full color-scale of nature may be divided into four octaves, of which less than one-quarter is taken up by the prismatic scale of the rainbow, which includes all the colors visible to the human eye. Immediately below the line of infrared, at the point where the human vision ceases to record color-impressions, there begins a series of vibrations which we can only feel as warmth; and still lower down the scale is another series which the human ear records in the form of sound. Yet we know of a certainty that these vibrations are also potential color-waves, that each note of music carries its own special color-note, whose quality and beauty, alas! may never be known to man, owing to the limited range of his vision.

However, no one can with certainty affirm that this may not be one of the joys that await future generations. Nothing is beyond the range of possibility. Already, by means of the fluoroscope, we are able to extend our vision somewhat, and peer over a little into the realm of the ultraviolet. And, if it is held that a wise providence, at the beginning of things, limited our sensory nerves to the record of such impressions as were essential to the physical existence of the primal creature, thereby confining our later aesthetic activities to the exploitation of a given range of sensations, a certain regret is nevertheless permissible when one thinks of the bewildering color-feast that might await us in a Wagner overture or a Beethoven sonata. What a fascinating problem it would be, for instance, to work out the color probabilities of some great masterpiece of music, and fling them glowing upon the translucent page of a vast cathedral window. If the time ever comes when man is able, by means of some miraculous transformer, to gaze upon music-color, it is safe to venture the prediction that it will be found to be harmonious and beautiful in proportion to the harmony and beauty of the music upon which it is based.

This is guesswork, of course, but it rests upon a strong basis of probability. Our actual knowledge of the subject is at present limited to mathematics. The velocity of the impulses has been noted and the number of the vibrations has been counted. We know those of sound to be comparatively slow, there being but 4,000 vibrations to the inch in the highest treble note of the piano. Above this on the ascending scale comes a long series of vibrations of which we know little or nothing; and it is not until we reach 36,000 vibrations to the inch that we come again within the range of human sensory consciousness. This number represents the rate of vibrations in the red note of our prismatic scale. The rate of vibration increases throughout the scale until with the ultraviolet it reaches 61,000 to the inch. Here we step out once more into the unknown.

Yet color has no actual existence. It is only by courtesy that we can use the word. Nature is a monochrome save when there are living eyes to see it. The trees are not really green, nor are the flowers red and yellow and blue. Each object simply reflects rays of light which vibrate at a given rate of speed; and these rays, smiting upon the sensitive retina of the eye, produce the impressions which we know as color. Were it not for the retina there would be no color; and when the sensory nerves of the retina are partially paralyzed or deficient, as in the case of the color-blind, nature appears to the eye in her true monochromatic garb.

The human eye resembles closely the photographic camera, both in structure and in its manner of functioning. At the front in both is placed the lens, with its diaphragm to control the quantity of light which enters the recording chamber, this function being performed in the human eye by the elastic iris, which contracts and expands automatically as the light waxes or wanes. At the back of the camera is the sensitized plate, and at the back of the eye is the infinitely more sensitive retina, overlaid by the optic nerve, with its millions upon millions of minute tentacles, reaching out to seize upon every fleeting color and form that passes before the lens. These little transparent filaments (so infinitely minute that the point of the finest needle is like a fence-post in comparison) are divided into two distinct varieties, known respectively as rods and cones. The rods are straight and pointed like needles, and the cones are somewhat blunt at the extremity.

We are told that the number of these nerve filaments reaches the astonishing total of about 137,000,000, of which only 7,000,000 are cones; but it is with this comparatively insignificant number of 7,000,000 cones that we artists have particularly to do. It is the function of the cones to record color, while the needles take care of the light.

If each of us had only received the 7,000,000 cones which are his just due, all would be well. Unfortunately, this is not the case. Nature abhors a duplicate, and no two human beings are similarly endowed in this respect. To the favored few she has given an unfair share of the precious cones, and others she has deprived of their birthright. The fortunate ones are the great colorists of the world, while those bereft are the color-blind.

Now we, as artists, could afford to ignore all this scientific side of the color question, were it not for the fact that it makes clear certain things which it is well for us to know. In the first place, it shows us the futility of any serious attempt to cultivate the sense of color. We are born with a certain given number of color-cones, and with just that allotment we must be content to go through life, for there is no known way of increasing their number, or of augmenting their efficiency. This efficiency may be decreased, however, either by a sudden shock, by paralysis, or by abuse of tobacco. In partial compensation for the depression born of the knowledge of this ruthless law, is the further knowledge that the artistic personality of a painter must be chiefly credited to the working of this same law – for our sense of color is primarily due to the varying number of color-cones with which each of us is endowed. It is in color, more than in any other artistic attribute, that the temperamental quality of a painter's product shows itself most clearly.

In more than the strictly scientific sense heretofore noted, color is very closely allied to music. Both are sensuous and passional, playing directly upon the emotions and producing their effects by some mysterious appeal to the subconscious, whose ways have as yet eluded us. Both, in their highest expression, come nearer to the perfect ideal of beauty as felt and understood by humanity than any other form of art. Finally, both are stimulating and mentally suggestive, while attempting no direct intellectual expression; and this is the test of the highest form of art – that it should stimulate the imagination and suggest more than it expresses. This emotional attribute of color is keenly felt even in a work of art as devoid of any intellectual appeal, as a Turkish rug or a Japanese ceramic; but when color is used purposely to enhance and offset some poetic mood of nature, as in a Venetian sunset by Gedney Bunce, or a spring morning by Corot, its poignant charm is overpowering and irresistible. It is hardly necessary to say, however, that it requires the intuitive genius of the master to accomplish this result with certainty. Those of us who are gifted only with the average, normal color-sense, cannot hope to rise to similar heights; but we can nevertheless learn something from the great ones – if not how to climb the heights, at least how to avoid the pitfalls. Where the color-sense is not infallible, for instance, it is safe to avoid the brilliant tones, to deal in a gamut of quiet and delicate hues. I have a friend who, though color-blind, is a clever and successful painter. His pictures sell well, and I doubt if one of his patrons has ever guessed that he must label the red and the green on his palette in order to tell them apart. Discovering his misfortune only after several years of study, he determined to see if by limiting his palette to the scale of yellows, blues, and grays in which his sight was normal, adding only a little touch of red or green here and there to heighten the effect, he might not still produce creditable pictures. He was, fortunately, a good draughtsman, with a fine sense of the picturesque in his arrangement of mass and values. For his specialty he wisely chose townscapes and street scenes, thus eliminating altogether the dangerous problems of the greens; and his success (for he has taken many medals and received many honors) shows at least how much may be accomplished by pure intelligence in the avoidance of insurmountable obstacles and difficulties.

Another useful point that we may learn is the emotional effect of the different colors. The warm colors, the yellow, red, and orange, are always exciting, stimulating, sometimes irritating, and in the end fatiguing. Red, as is well known, always enrages a bull; and in a lesser degree it affects other animals and birds in the same way. A red skirt floating in the wind is the best protection to the poultry-yard, for the chicken-hawk will never approach it. With man the stimulating effect of this color appears to be pleasantly exciting rather than disagreeable when taken in moderation; but did a wrathful deity desire to punish mankind with a specially hideous form of torture, I could imagine nothing more dreadful than that he should change all the green in the world into screaming scarlet. Imagine a bright vermilion world under a brilliant sun, and tell me how long it would be before all the inhabitants would be raving maniacs.

The cool colors – blue, green, mauve, violet, and all the delicate intervening grays – are, on the contrary, restful colors in the emotional sense; and the wisdom of the choice of these tones for the landscape scheme of the world is hardly open to question. Moreover, it is well known to all expert household decorators that these tones are always the most satisfactory for the walls and all large spaces in interior decoration; and that the powerful notes of red, yellow, and orange should come in only as a spot here and there to enliven the effect. If we carry the same idea into the domain of purely pictorial art, we shall see how the restful beauty of a gray-green landscape by Corot is enhanced by the tiny red bonnet of his peasant woman.

While it is, alas! only too true that any personal and individual progress in the domain of color is debarred by physical law, it is nevertheless a fact that in the broad and world-wide sense, most of the progress made in art in the past two centuries has been made in the domain of color. For one thing, we have in the meantime moved out of doors. From the quiet, subdued, and restful light of the studio, we have stepped out into the gay and palpitating sunlight; and in so doing we have had to meet and conquer many new and fascinating problems, problems whose fundamental color scheme is the reverse of the one which had for a thousand years engrossed the attention of the older artists. In the quiet north light of the studio, illumined only by the sky, the lights were cool and the shadows warm; in the open air, on the contrary, the lights are warm and the shadows cool, for out here in the open the gay yellow sunlight is the source of illumination, while the shadows catch only the cool reflections of the sky. At the present time it is hard to conceive how difficult it was for the first landscape painters to make this simple change in their point of view, how tenacious the old tradition of the studio proved to be, and how very slowly it was abandoned to make room for the simple truths of out-of-door nature. Even after the new law had been fully recognized and accepted, the *methods* of the older masters were adhered to. So great and true a colorist as Corot, even, continued to "rub in" his shadows in the warm browns of the sixteenth century painters. Of course, this "rub in" was later painted over with the violet and pearl-gray tones of outdoor nature, but the brown underlay has begun to "strike through" in many of his pictures, and it may in the end seriously impair some of them. It was not until the "luminarists" came along with their gay and militant iconoclasm that the old tradition was wholly cast aside, and the pearly stream of outdoor color at last flowed pure and free and undefiled. And if it happens (as it very well may) that we shall also cast aside the luminarists' patchwork system of prismatic spots and splashes, we shall nevertheless be eternally their debtors in that they freed us from the fetters that bound us to the old system of indoor painting, and gave us a fresh palette of pearl and opal and lapis lazuli, in place of the old snuff-colored affair of our fathers. Thanks to them, it is not possible for the worst of our modern landscapists to use such distressing color as is to be found in the best of the Hobbemas and Cuyps and Ruysdaels of the sixteenth century.

What developments in the direction of color the future may hold in store for us, it is of course difficult to say. One thing, however, is sure; the mathematics which govern the laws of color will be worked out and tabulated, as have those relating to music; so that it will be possible and easy for anyone, either expert or layman, to produce a harmony in color by the simple application of the prescribed formula. But beyond this the mathematicians' contributions to art will have little value. Its direct benefits will be found to be negative rather than positive. While it may prevent the perpetration of jarring discords, it will hardly make possible the creation of masterpieces; for here again the personal equation comes into play. Lacking the note of personality, no real art is possible. A musician of my acquaintance, having discovered that when the law of mathematics was applied to a sonata by Beethoven, the theme worked out faultlessly to a seemingly inevitable conclusion, decided that the process could be reversed, and that a given theme, if correctly figured out, would undoubtedly produce a musical number of faultless beauty. He put his theory into practice and made a sonata according to this system. His production was impeccable – and absolutely worthless. When will the world learn that art cannot be manufactured?

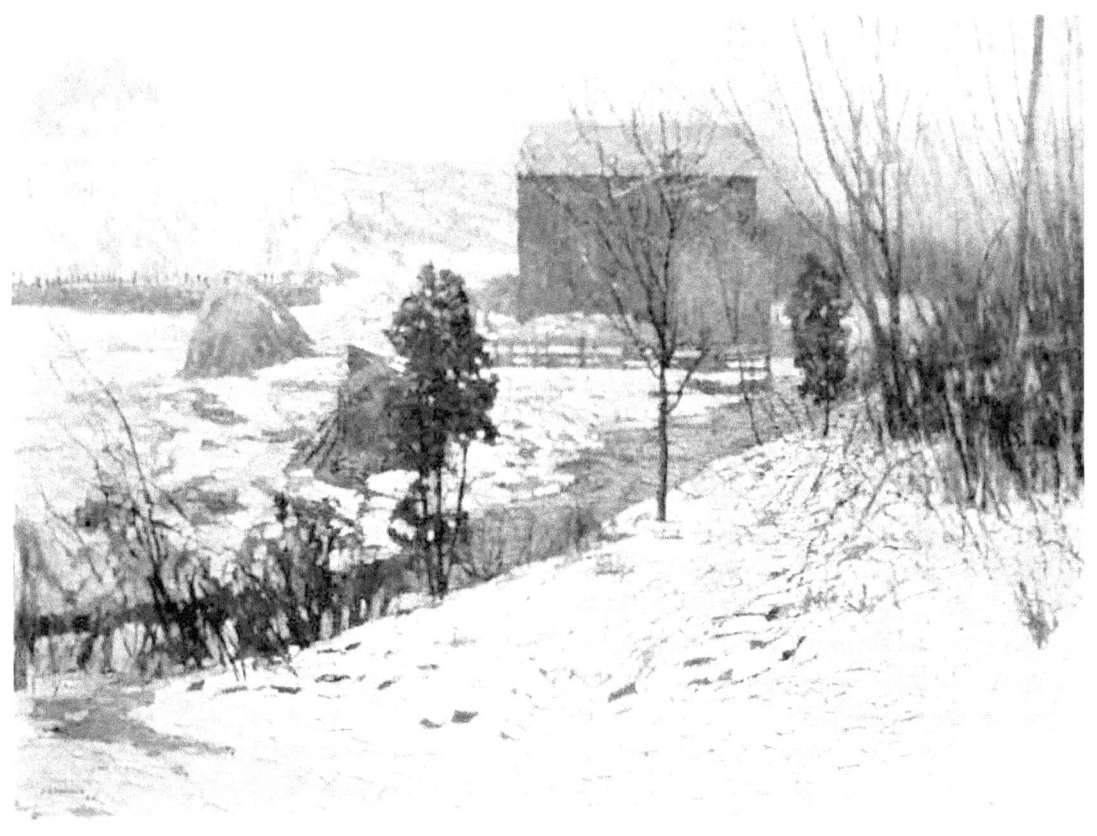

E. W. Redfield
The Red Barn

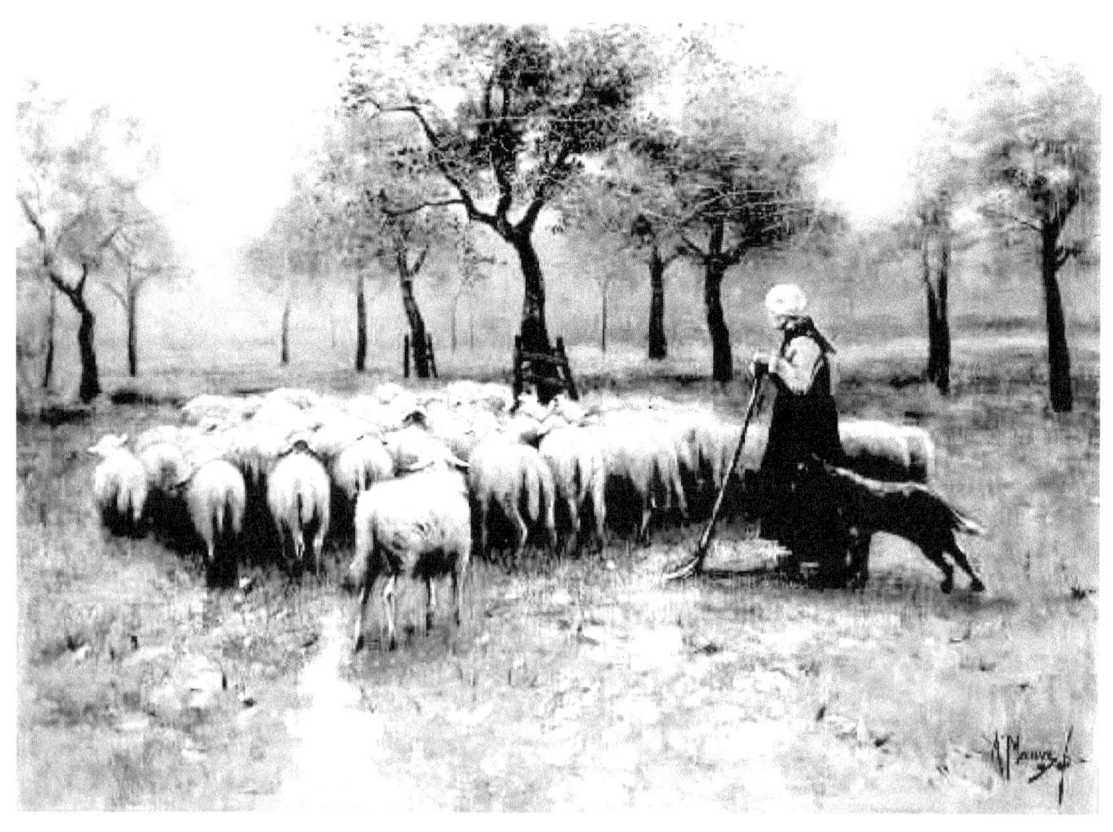

Anton Mauve
A Flock of Sheep

·III·

Vibration

The most splendid achievement of the nineteenth century in painting, and its best legacy to the future, was the discovery of the technical means by which the scintillating effect of living light could be transferred to the dead and rigid surface of a canvas. Of this the old masters had absolutely no conception. The discovery belongs to our generation, and is a distinction of which any age might well be proud – for it is the only important step in advance made since the great Renaissance of the fifteenth century. Without it landscape art had hardly been possible – landscape art, that is, in the modern sense in which we know it. There were indeed many landscape painters among the older masters – Ruysdael and Cuyp, Hobbema, Salvator Rosa, Claude, and even Rembrandt on occasion. But, owing to a curious psychological phenomenon, none of these men were able to see straight out of their eyes once they were in the open air. They painted landscape, but landscape in which the fields and the hills and the trees bore no relation to the skies that overhung them, in which the shadows were warmer in color than the lights, in which browns took the place of violets, and in which (owing to ignorance of the laws of vibration) the surface of the canvas never entirely disappeared from view.

As I have previously stated, the dawn of the new movement was seen in England, when Constable and his confreres carried their easels into the open, and brought back studies wherein the pearly tones of out-of-door nature were for the first time accurately seen and noted.

A few of these pictures finding their way to France, were eagerly studied by a group of young Frenchmen, who, tired of the hide-bound conventions of David and Delaroche, were quick to recognize and absorb the new light. Armed with this fresh knowledge, these men in their turn went out into the fields, and looked and studied and painted; and thus grew up the great school of Barbizon.

A little later the artistic world was startled by the appearance of the French impressionists or luminarists. According to them, nature had spread her palette upon the heavens in the form of the rainbow, where all who looked might see and understand it. And everywhere and always, on hill and dale, on rock and tree, so long as light endured there must also be the rainbow – attenuated and diminished in power, it is true, but with its three primary and prismatic colors, locking and interlocking, shifting and shimmering and playing across one another in an iridescent dance of color that was, or should be, always clearly visible to the eye of the trained artist. And as they saw nature so these men painted their pictures, laying the pure pigments side by side upon the canvas in strokes and dots or dashes of red and yellow and blue which, seen at the proper distance, were supposed to fuse into the desired tones and masses, while at the same time retaining a luminous quality of their own never before seen upon canvas.

I can remember the first exhibition which these men gave in Paris in the little rotunda behind the Palais de I'Industrie; and the bewilderment and scorn with which it was received by the critics and the older painters. I can remember also the heroic struggle which they made against apparently hopeless odds; and we all know how they finally won the long fight, proving their point so conclusively that no one today thinks of questioning it.

But while all painters now admit that the prismatic theory of light as applied to the art of painting is both scientifically correct and artistically admirable – that it is practically impossible to secure luminosity in a picture without some sacrifice to the principle, it is nevertheless open to question if the crude and primitive method invented by the French Impressionists is necessarily the last word on the technical side of the matter. We must have "vibration" in a picture, it is true, because without vibration there can be no light, but may it not be possible to secure the necessary vibration without loss of "quality," that charm of surface with which we would not willingly part?

There are many, many paths by which the problem may be approached. Indeed, one of the chief delights of the art of painting lies in the fact that each artist does, and of necessity must, invent his own technique; for his personal technique is an inalienable part of the personal vision which makes his art his own. Nevertheless there are in a broad sense only four general methods of painting with oil colors, from which (used either in their direct and simple expression or infinitely varied and compounded) all of our personal technical methods must be drawn. First we may mention the method used by so many of the old masters, which consisted in a solid underpainting in black and white with a slight admixture of red. In this method the whole scheme of the picture was built up with these three pigments, and all of the drawing and modelling was accomplished without any attempt at color. Then, after a very thorough drying, the work was completed and the color obtained by a series of very thin glazes drawn over the dried and hardened surface. This method, although wonderfully sound in itself and lasting in its results, must of course be discarded by the modern painter for the reason that it precludes all possibility of vibration.

Of the three remaining systems one other is entirely bad for the same reason – it does away with vibration. This system consists in mixing the tones evenly and applying them to the canvas in smooth flat masses in much the same manner as a house painter paints his door or cornice. There remain then practically but two systems from which the modern painter is at liberty to choose. The first of these is the spot and dash method used by the Impressionists and their school. It must be clear to anyone that this system, while giving beautiful results in the way of luminosity, does not logically follow the forms of nature, or reproduce her surfaces, and it must therefore be regarded as an imperfect and a temporary manner which is destined to be superseded in time by some more supple and expressive technique.

The last of the four systems mentioned and one which has gradually come to be adopted by the vast majority of our best landscape painters is one in which vibration is obtained by means of a cool overtone painted freshly into a warm undertone, care being taken not to mix or blend the two coats and not to cover up completely the undertone, rather letting it show through brokenly all over the canvas; the vibration being secured, naturally, by the separate play of the warm and the cold notes. Neither alone would accomplish this purpose, nor would the neutral gray that would result from a too thorough mixing of the tones in the final brushwork.

This method has first of all the great advantage of being thoroughly logical; for in nature herself the undertones are represented by the local color of the various units – leaves, grass, rocks, and good rich earth; and these are always warmer and more vivid in color than the lights dropped upon their surfaces by the over-arching sky. But the method has the still greater advantage of being wonderfully supple and responsive lending itself not only to the infinite variations of technique demanded by differing temperament in the artist, but allowing endless latitude for any and all desired changes in composition or mass after the picture is placed on the canvas; for all of these changes can be made in the undertone itself before the overtone is applied, and therefore before any attempt to secure vibration has been made. Indeed the whole picture in all its exact values can and should be built up in this preliminary covering of the canvas, for the value of the overtone must in every case exactly match the *value* of the undertone. While we wish to secure broken color, we must avoid broken values, for they utterly destroy atmosphere. Anyone who wishes to prove this to his own satisfaction can readily do so by making the following experiment. Paint a sunny sky in two simple tones, using, say, delicate gray pink for the underlay and blue green or green blue for the overlay, varying the color from the horizon up as it occurs in nature. In the first experiment mix the overlay with extreme care until its value exactly matches that of the underlay. Then mix another lot to the green blue either slightly darker or slightly lighter than the underlay. Apply these tones each to one-half of the prepared sky, and you will find that the sky painted with the perfectly matched tone will flyaway infinitely, will be bathed in a perfect atmosphere, while the other half of the canvas will remain merely paint and canvas, and will have no atmospheric quality whatever. The explanation of this is very simple – nature deals in broken color everywhere, but she never deals in broken values. The color dances, but the values "stay put."

As to the general tint of color of the undertone no rule can be given, for it can never in any two pictures be alike. It will vary infinitely, according to the effect to be painted, and also according to the temperament of the artist. There would seem to be only two rules that cannot be broken: first the undertone *must* be warmer than the overtone, and second it must *never* be brown; and this for the excellent reason that out-of-door nature abhors brown, and never uses it. Even the house-painter's most venomous effort in this direction is generally met by kindly and all-forgiving mother nature with some gray reflection from the sky to mitigate its worst virulence. The one weak spot in the technical armor of the

Barbizon painters was their tenacity in clinging to the traditional recipe of the brown rub-in. And although this was allowed to dry thoroughly and was then completely painted over with pearly tones that were true to nature, the browns are now beginning to strike through to the surface – to the serious detriment of some of the finest pictures on earth.

Now when the fullest acknowledgment has been made of our stupendous indebtedness to the discoverers of prismatic painting, it will be wise for us to recognize the limitations of the system; to admit that there are very many effects in which it must be used with extreme caution, and others in which it had best not be employed at all. If we frankly envisage the fact that its chief function is to endow our dead pigments with life, with the power to convey in a picture the joyous impression of dancing light, we shall understand where these limitations begin. As the system gives its best results in the translation of brilliant sunlight, so, as the light decreases its value decreases, until in a low-toned moonlight it may become positively detrimental. It can easily be seen that in this subdued light the sibilant vibration of powerful color-tones would be fatally out of place and their use detract seriously from the brooding sense of mystery which gives to night its most poignant charm.

We must not forget, moreover, that another weakness inherent to the system lies in the physical impossibility of securing with pigments and brushes any approximation to the infinitely fine and delicate color vibration of nature – where no spot or dash or stroke of pure color is anywhere visible; and that our best efforts in this direction are therefore only a compromise – that owing to this compromise our best technique of vibration remains at the present time more or less obtrusive, and that any technique which obtrudes itself is to that extent bad technique; for technique, as Millet so truly said, "should always hide itself modestly behind the thing to be expressed."

Finally let us frankly admit the fact that vibration has little to do with atmosphere in a picture (in spite of much wordy argument to the contrary). A Whistler nocturne, for instance, which is painted without the slightest vibration, or any attempt at broken color, may swoon in the most exquisite bath of atmosphere, while a vibrant Monet, *with a few hard edges*, may lack all atmospheric quality.

Atmosphere in a painting is only secured by the use (conscious or unconscious) of the laws of "refraction," a much more subtle and elusive visual phenomenon of which I will say a word in the following chapter.

·IV·

Refraction

What is refraction – refraction as applied to art? When I first had to speak to my own students of this most elusive but most important quality, I found myself curiously handicapped by the fact that there was no word in the English language to describe it. A careful search of the dictionaries revealed nothing that met the need. The French word *envelope* and our own "lost-edge" were descriptive of the result only and not of the cause. Neither radiation, nor reaction, nor reflection, nor ambience fully defined the thing which it was desired to describe.

Piracy seemed the only way out of the dilemma; so I boldly seized upon the word refraction and forced it willy-nilly to assume the new role. And while it was necessary to twist it far from its original meaning I have faith that with growing years it will come to carry gracefully the full burden of definition.

For the purposes of this paper therefore the reader will kindly assume refraction to stand for that intimate effect of one mass of color or value upon its adjoining mass which results in the "lost-edge," and a general diffusion of tone, thus giving to pictures their atmospheric quality.

Now refraction is only in a very limited sense an objective fact. It is mainly a *visual* fact whose operation is due to the imperfect construction of the lens of the human eye. The scientific fact is that the edges of things are sharp and hard as a rule. This is amply proved by the photographic lens, which gives us a clear-cut definition all over the plate which the human eye could never hope to compass in looking at nature through its own imperfect instrument. And if the camera were still more perfect, if there were no question of focus, it would probably give us an edge everywhere as sharp as the traditional Toledo blade.

But this scientific fact would still remain an artistic lie. Fortunately, we painters have to do only with *impressions* and not with realities. For these impressions we must rely solely upon the lenses which God has given us; and as a painter I congratulate myself daily that the lens of the human eye was designed not at all after the pattern of the lenses adapted to the camera, the microscope, and the various other scientific instruments. As we are now provided, nature is infinitely beautiful to us; while it might have been a hideous nightmare of sharp and cutting angles or edges, without rest or relief anywhere.

It is not necessary for our purposes to enter here into the physiological structure of the human eye. It will be enough to state that its radius of exact vision is extremely limited; so limited in fact that at a distance of six feet from the eye it would hardly be possible for any human being to enumerate accurately the spots on a target four feet in diameter, while holding the gaze rigidly fixed on the bull's-eye. Beyond the radius of twelve inches from the centre the image begins to blur, and this blur increases rapidly, until out of the tail of the eye on either side we get only an in definite consciousness of things rather than any genuine vision of things themselves.

It is curious when you come to think of it, how many untold centuries it has taken mankind to recognize this simple visual phenomenon, which everyone of the race must have been experiencing ten thousand times a day for ten million years; and how few there are even today who are fully cognizant of it.

A gentleman of marked intelligence and culture once berated me for what he termed the artist's impudence in giving to the public a smudge of greenish brown or of gray up against the sky and asking them to accept it as a tree. "Why," he said, "I can see every leaf on that oak tree in the meadow yonder. And so can anyone whose eyesight is normal."

My reply to this was to pin a card to one of the oak's lower branches and ask my friend, standing at ten paces, to tell me how many of the leaves he could count without shifting his gaze from the white card.

"Well, by Jove!" he presently exclaimed, "I can't count up to fifty."

"What do the rest of the leaves look like," I asked, "a more or less indefinite blur?"

"Yes! Just a blur." "Well," I said, "now you understand just a little of the meaning of the word refraction."

But the new knowledge did not seem to console him. He continued to regret the loss of all those leaves. I could not convince him that it would have been a disaster had he been *obliged* to see each individual leaf of all the millions which the tree doubtless carried, and in addition to this, to be conscious of all the twigs and blades of grass and other infinite details around about.

Now any interesting picture motive generally has a focus, or centre of interest on which the artist's eye rests with especial pleasure; and in view of the visual limitation just described it is evident that this portion will appear much more definite in outline than the outlying regions of the composition; which will become more and more blurred, as they recede, with the softened or lost edge everywhere. This is refraction; and as the eye sees it, so, without question, the hand should paint it.

But there are other motives – certain of Whistler's nocturnes, for instance – wherein the eye broods dreamily over the whole scene, not resting fixed upon any one given point of interest; and these should be painted precisely as Whistler painted them, the refraction distributed evenly all over the canvas. Whistler, in fact, was past master of the art of refraction, its one great and supreme prophet; and it is to the consummate and most artistic use which he made of this one quality that his work owes all of that emotional, appealing, and poetic charm which is its distinguishing trait.

Of course every artist of any training at the present day is more or less aware of this phenomenon, otherwise his pictures would not find acceptance at the hands of the juries, for they would be hopelessly hard and edgy and un-atmospheric. No one, for instance, would today think of painting the spots of sky showing through the interstices of a large tree with the tint he had mixed for the sky out in the open on the other side of the picture. If he did so paint these spots, they would shine out like electric lights and he would instinctively lower their value at once. Here the law of refraction has come into force again, and the visual no longer accords with the actual. The sky behind the tree of course is in reality just as light as the rest of the sky, but the refraction from the surrounding dark mass of foliage has robbed the spots of much of their power of light and has softened them in every way.

But while all good painters today are aware of refraction, and (whether consciously or unconsciously) use it in their work, very few, I think, have any conception of the far-reaching effect and control of the law. I am myself absolutely convinced that the refraction emanating, we will say, from a large dark tree standing up against a sunset sky will affect the sky and gradually lower its value out to its very centre; and that, *per contra*, the darkest spot in the tree itself will be found to be near its focal point, owing to the inward refraction from the sky – for naturally refraction acts both ways, from light to dark as well as from dark to light. Whether it is necessary or advisable in practical painting to utilize the law up to the extreme limit, is of course a point that is open to discussion. As painters our business is to transmit to picture-lovers through the medium of our pictures the emotions, and the impressions of strength and power, or of poetic beauty which have come to us direct from nature; but in doing this we are not called upon to saddle ourselves with more difficulties than are absolutely necessary. Indeed it is by means of the wise selection and synthesis of the elements which are *essential* to his work and the ruthless elimination of all such as are unessential that the consummate artist shows his calibre. Nevertheless I can recall certain canvases by Corot, poetic masterpieces of the first order, in which the very fullest use of this law was made. It can do no harm at least for any painter to keep the law always in mind, to be used whenever its use will add an element of beauty or of distinction to his work.

In addition to the above defined theory, a long and close study of the law of refraction has left on my mind the strong conviction that the out-worn and rather cheap practice of vignetting was not without a certain sound basis of justification in the underlying laws of nature. If you will bear in mind the fact that the colors and values that are seen out of the corners of the eyes, are, on account of their very situation, able to affect only a very limited number of the sensitive nerves of the retina, you will understand that the force of their impact must be proportionately less than those which come to the eye from the full centre of vision; and if you are willing to try the experiment of looking for five minutes at a given scene in nature, keeping the gaze fixed during all that time on some focal point – a church steeple, for instance – but throwing the *mind's* eye constantly back and forth from outside margin to centre and from centre to outside margin again, it will gradually dawn upon you that there is an actual and very marked visual difference in the color and value intensity of the two radii. I am sure, therefore, that the eighteenth-century artists who made use of this law in their work were fundamentally correct in their intuitions; but the excess to which they carried it landed them in the quagmire of the commonplace and vulgar. Nevertheless, I am certain that no picture in its extreme corners should be painted with quite the same vigor of technique or strength of color or of value as in its natural focal centre. Indeed, a careful study of certain masterpieces shows that wonderful results have occasionally been obtained by the reserved and masterly use of this principle. In the "Shepherdess," by Millet, for instance, the sense of immensity and of limitless space which marks and distinguishes that great canvas is derived largely from the extremely subtle use to which he put his knowledge of this obscure phenomenon.

So far I have spoken of refraction only in its relation to values. But there is also color refraction; and here its action is much more in harmony with the scientific laws of color, for its first and immediate effect is to call up the complementary. I sat one day out in the blazing sunlight on the white painted deck of a river steamer holding in my hand a crimson ticket, in the centre of which a square hole had been perforated. After glancing through this hole for an instant I handed the ticket to my companion and asked her to say what color the deck appeared to be as seen through the square opening. "Why! it is brilliant green," she replied, at the same time putting the ticket aside to see if in reality the deck had been painted green in that particular spot.

This, of course, was an extreme case; the very powerful scarlet, under the compelling stress of the intense sunlight, had simply conjured up its complementary in an exceptionally brilliant and dramatic demonstration. But in greater or less degree, the law is always at work. Any painter who has posed his sitter against a red background, for instance, must have noted how the red ground brought out the green tones in the flesh. And has it ever occurred to you why never a portrait was painted against a bright blue background. Simply because there has never been found a human being modest enough to stand for the jaundiced presentment of himself that would be the natural result – yellow being the complementary of blue.

It results from this that no color has any definite and fixed existence of its own – once it is out of the tube. It is changed and varied infinitely as its surroundings change and vary. Even when it is fixed definitely under the varnish of some masterpiece, it remains subject to the same old law, and, to a certain extent, can be made attractive and lovely, or forbidding and ugly according to the background against which the picture is hung.

Of course in the scale of subdued colors color-refraction works feebly, and it is therefore of minor importance to the landscape painter, though, as I have already noted, Corot knew how to make good use of the little crimson cap on his peasant women; for the tiny spot of red doubled the beauty of his delicate greens. But the figure painter occasionally finds a knowledge of this law of great value; as, for instance, when he wishes to play upon the emotions by the simple use of pure color. Splendid effects have been produced in this way by Monticelli, by Frank Brangwyn, and more recently by the Spaniard Sorolla.

It is fortunate, perhaps, that the limits of space here draw a line, for the things that might be said about refraction are endless. I will, however, add one parting word in regard to *its technical side*. How may we best secure the lost-edge and the other qualities deriving from refraction while maintaining crisp drawing and a free and agreeable brushwork. In this we can hardly do better than study and follow the two great masters of the art, Corot and Whistler. Prepare for the refraction, as they did, by lowering values as you approach the edge, so that the final stroke which draws your limb or your tree may be as fresh and as crisp as possible without being hard; and if you are painting in broken color – that is, using prismatic vibration to secure luminosity – then do all this preparatory work fully and carefully in the undertone, so that the final painting may be accomplished with that dash and freedom which, say what you may, will always remain an admirable quality in a picture.

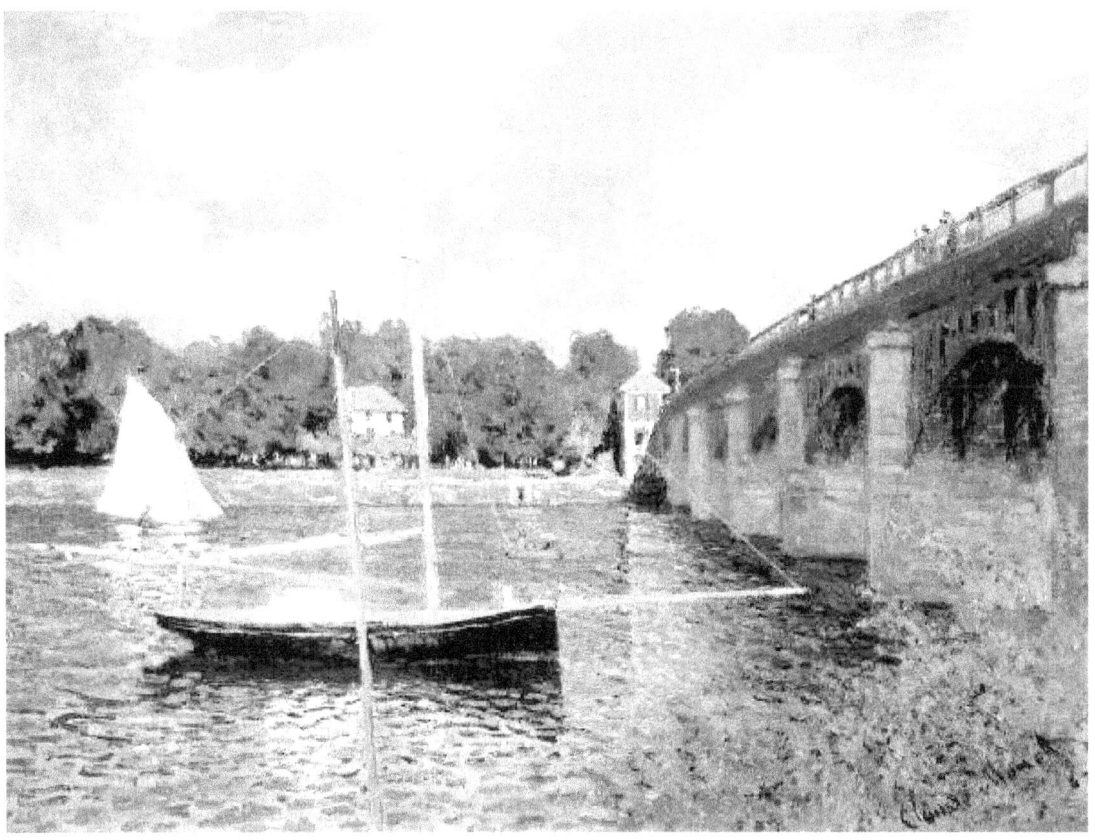

Claude Monet
The Highway Bridge at Argenteuil

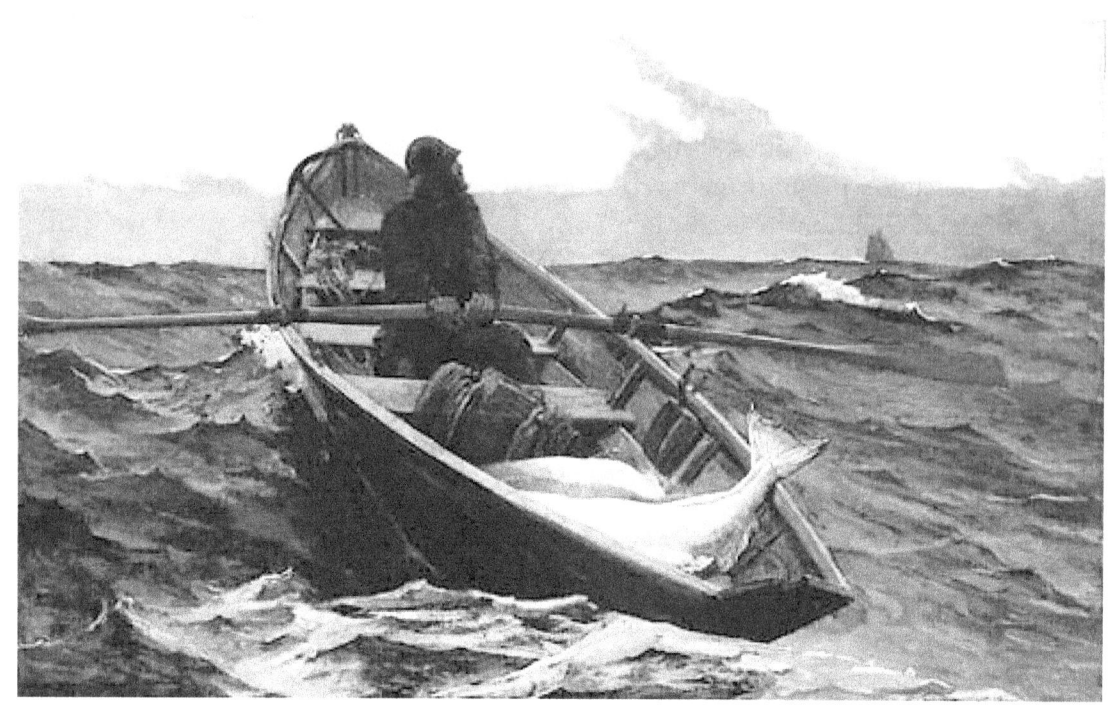

Winslow Homer
The Fog Warning

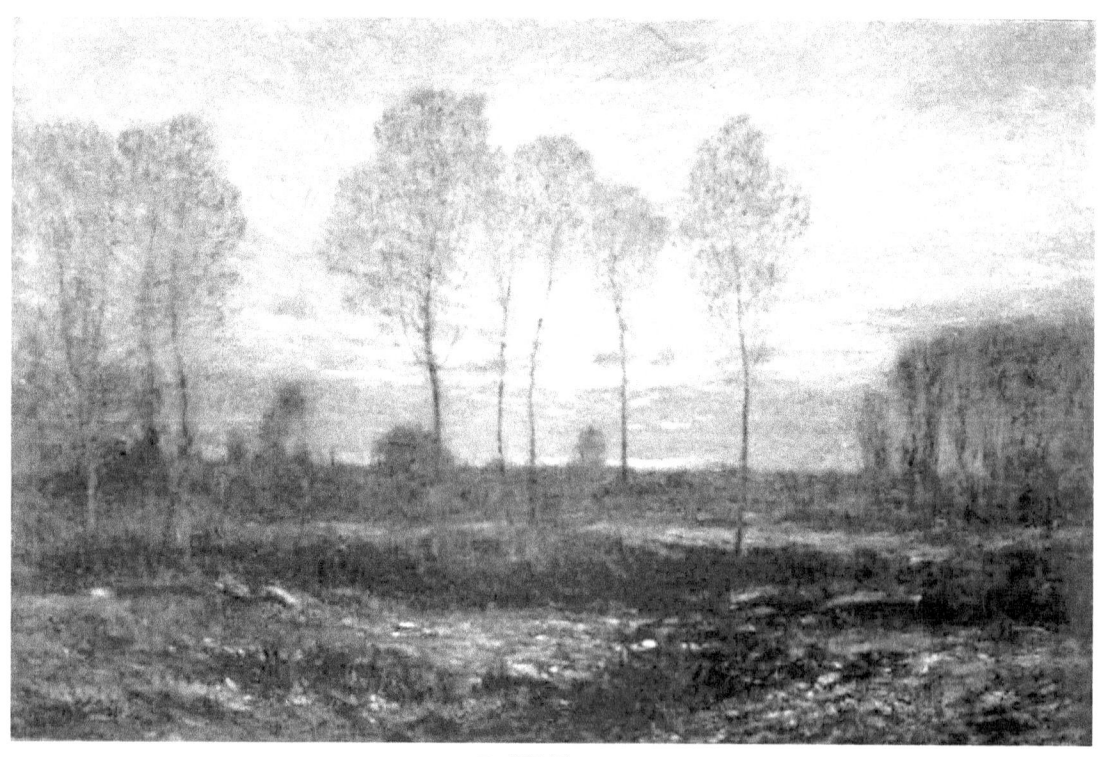

D.W. Tryon
Twilight Autumn

·V·

Values

O f late years the English term "values" has entirely replaced the Italian "chiaroscuro" by which painters were long wont to describe the light and shade of a picture as apart from its color. The change is certainly a good one.

Values are a pure convention, because they are built upon the assumption that nature is monochromatic. They are however, a most important convention – one that is practically indispensable to a painter – for it is upon sound values that pictures depend for their solidity and their convincing power. Good painting, after all, is a matter of analysis and synthesis; and we painters are so used to picking nature to pieces, studying her in detail, considering the undertones by themselves, for instance, while we hold the overtones in abeyance, that we find no difficulty in separating the chiaroscuro from the color, and temporarily assuming a color blindness if we have it not.

But values are a convention in still another sense. Our ability to counterfeit nature in a picture depends upon a palette made up of a certain number of dead pigments, whose scale of light and shade is ludicrously inadequate when compared with that of nature. Limited thus on the material side, the best we can do is to *translate* the infinite value scale of nature into our sadly finite scale of pigments, and endeavor, by most careful balance, to adjust our means to our ends. This would be practically impossible were it not for the kindly help we receive from the human imagination, which is ever ready to accept a mere hint and build upon it a whole world; to fill in all discrepancies; and, given a few scratches of pen or pencil, to construct therefrom a complete representation of nature. How peculiarly human is this mental attitude is proved by the fact that no animal is ever known to recognize the most realistic painting as anything more than simple paint and canvas.

Contenting ourselves, however, with our own small value-scale, as we needs must, and assuming it to be adequate, the most important thing to consider is the value-*key* of our picture. Assuming the whole scale of values from the deepest black to the purest white to be represented by the number 100, the question arises as to what proportion of this number we shall use in the particular work which we are proposing to execute. In this matter the golden rule is *reserve*. We lose rather than gain in power by forcing the note, and a picture in which the whole scale from black to white should be employed would be absolutely without atmosphere, and without charm. It would indeed be a crudity and a horror, from which we would flee with hands on high. The whole beauty of a canvas depends often on the wisdom with which we make this choice of key – whether our picture is pitched in the upper, the middle, or the lower register, and whether we use a limited or an extended scale.

It is evident, of course, that we *could* attenuate our scale to the vanishing point, so that a breath would almost blow the picture from the canvas; just as by going to the other extreme we should fatally brutalize the work.

But within the limits of, say, the number ten and the number ninety of the scale, there exist a dozen or more keys of value, anyone of which we are at liberty to select. It is equally evident that a picture painted in any one of these keys would be true to nature, if the relative values within the scale were carefully noted and adhered to. But in every case there would be *one* of those keys which would have suited the mood of that particular picture better than any other, and it is in the intuitive selection of just the right key that the true artist most frequently shows his power. As a rule, it may be said that the upper middle range will be found best to suit the great majority of pictures, but there are motives whose brilliancy calls out for the highest attainable key of light, and others whose brooding mystery must hide itself in the shadowy gloom of the lower register. Of equal importance with this question of altitude in the *register* is that of the numerical *scale* – whether to use ten, twenty, fifty, or seventy of the possible 100 points in the full scale. This will depend largely upon the effect to be produced, whether the message we have to convey is one of dramatic power, of brilliancy, or of tender and poetic charm. It will depend also considerably upon the character of the work and its ultimate destination. In a mural decoration, for instance, the demand for a restricted scale of values is absolutely mandatory, because the *first* consideration in a work of this character is that the observer must always remain conscious (or subconsciously conscious) of the flat surface of the wall. If this plane were destroyed, the architectural unity would suffer – the sense of the supporting power and strength of the wall being gone. In an easel picture it is just the contrary; there we desire to annihilate the flat surface of the canvas, to produce the illusion of atmosphere and to convey the impression that it would be possible to step over the border of the frame and out into the fields beyond. In this case therefore the scale of values must be generous enough to convey the impression of solidity and reality, while being held sufficiently in hand to obviate the danger of crudity.

As this whole question of values is a matter of *translation*, and of delicate adjustment inside of fixed conventional limits, there is practically no effect in nature that cannot at least be suggested by a wise and skilful use of pigments. Take, for instance, the familiar effect where the sun, high in the heavens, is reflected in a brilliant pathway of scintillating light across the surface of the sea. In this case it is evident that the actual color-scale of nature is a thousand times more powerful than that of the artist's palette; yet by a careful selection of the register, and a wise adjustment of the scale, it is quite possible not only to render the illusion of this radiant scene, but to do this without exhausting our limited value-scale. In fact, in this, and in all similar effects in which radiation of light is the principal motive of the picture, it is of the utmost importance to keep well within the limits of the scale, in order that even the deepest shadows shall remain luminous and palpitant. Nature *never* exhausts *her* value-scale. Even in the most violent effects, she always holds plenty in reserve. And, so far as is possible with our limited scale, we should do the same.

This, of course, does not mean that we should paint a gray-day landscape in a key so low that we could give its full force to a burst of sunlight that might suddenly strike across the scene. (If the sunlight is to be included, it should have been conceived as part of the picture in the beginning, and so arranged for). But it does mean that we should always be able to go a little higher on the high note or a little lower on the low note if it is desirable to do so.

Having decided upon the scale and the register, the next most important thing is so to visualize our subject that we shall be able to group our values in large and simple masses. See big! Grab the essential, and leave the little things for any foolish person who chooses to gather them up. To tell the truth, detail is so blatant, so insistent, that it takes years of hard training to see beyond it, to appreciate the essential bigness of things. This is particularly true of outdoor nature. The sun is a great leveller. It flattens all masses, the lights as well as the shadows. An outdoor picture motive is complicated indeed if it cannot be divided into four or five dominant values. If these are understood, and painted with sympathetic truth, it is astonishing how little detail it requires to complete the picture – the trunk of a tree, a few scattered leaves, the curve of a road, and the trick is turned. Always leave something to the imagination of the beholder. A picture is often complete long before you suspect it.

There is probably no better way of training the eye to simplicity of vision, than studying moonlight, for in moonlight effects, the broad masses alone are visible, and the shadows lie all over the picture in one big soft value. The lights are distributed in two or three values at most, and nowhere is there any detail. Try to see your daylight effects in the same way, and you will come far nearer the truth than you might think.

Personally, I am inclined to hold values to be the most important quality in a picture – and this in spite of the fact that the work must depend for its charm upon the other qualities of color, design, and refraction. But a picture that is good in all these respects being weak and unsound in values, will nevertheless be a poor picture. Values might be compared to the skeleton in a human figure, which depends for its beauty upon the exquisite curves of the rounded limbs, the silken sheen of the hair, and the color of eyes and lips and blushing cheeks. Remove the skeleton, and the whole fabric of beauty falls to earth a shapeless mass. Moreover, values are one of the few things in art that can be learned by almost anyone who is gifted with ordinary eyesight; and for that particular reason they should engage the earnest attention of every serious student. One who has thoroughly mastered them has gone a long way on the road to success in painting.

Of course, all that has here been said refers only to the art of the past and of the present, for it is by no means certain that the intellectual and spiritual conditions which now bind us will endure forever. When I try to draw aside the veil, and peer into the mists of the future, I seem to see another art, less material, more akin to the pure spirit of music; an art stripped of all that is gross and material; an art in which abstract beauty alone shall rule. In this new art values may very possibly be unnecessary, and all will be stated in terms of beautiful color.

This is not yet however; and any art which is to endure must be true to the spirit of its own age.

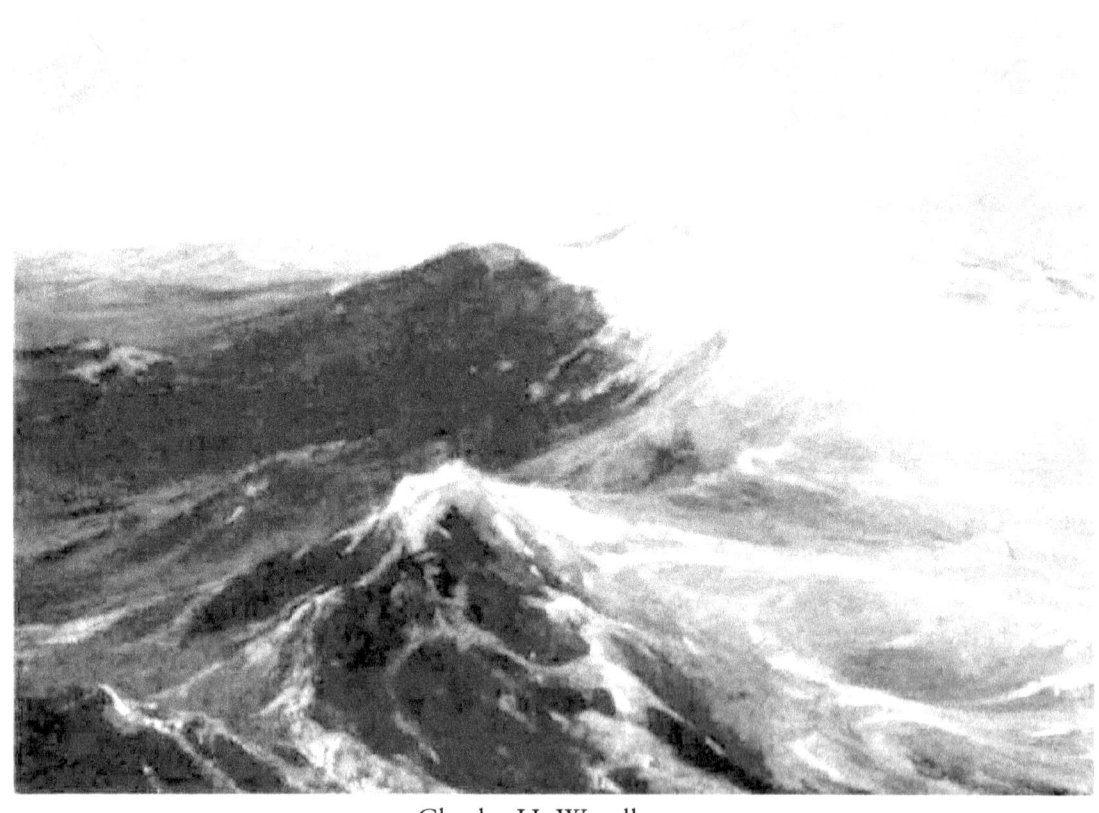

Charles H. Woodbury
The North Atlantic

·VI·

Drawing

Drawing is the grammar of art. As grammar is the framework on which all good literature is built, so drawing is the foundation of all good painting. It is no more possible to imagine a great picture with crude and incompetent drawing than it is to think of a great sonnet whose grammar should be uncouth and halting. Like grammar, also, drawing is not a virtue to be extolled in a picture, but an essential to be demanded.

Fortunately, both grammar and drawing may be learned by anyone of good average intelligence. In reference to drawing, however, this statement applies only to that kind of good, sound, commonplace drawing which serves to uphold a picture in which color and sentiment are the main things; but not, of course, to the truly great drawing which is beautiful in and by itself, and which is one of the rarest qualities in all art – so rare indeed that the great draughtsmen of the world can be counted upon the fingers of one hand. Of these probably Holbein and Leonardo were the most eminent examples. In the work of these two men the sense of refined and tender line was so exquisite that we should almost prefer to have it without color; and indeed when color was used to secure the added beauty of modelling, as in the "Mona Lisa," it was always flat and conventional. It would be impossible, for instance, to imagine a Holbein painted in the impressionist manner of the present day. The grace of line which is this master's chief distinction would be destroyed by the modern method of applying the pigment: and this shows once again the futility of the frequent demand that a single picture shall contain in itself all of the manifold qualities of art.

In landscape, of course, drawing is of secondary importance; color, refraction, and vibration ranking first; but no landscapist must imagine that for this reason a sound knowledge of drawing can be dispensed with. The character of his tree, his stream, his mountain outline is as important as the character of an eye or a mouth in a drawing of the human face. Moreover, a good knowledge of drawing is essential to good workmanship. The charm of a picture often lies in the freshness, the brilliancy, and alacrity of the brushwork; and this kind of stroke can only be secured when it is backed by a sure knowledge of the underlying form. The poor and uncertain draughtsman fumbling for form loses all "quality."

Turn the pages of any exhibition catalogue, and you will find it difficult to place your finger on the name of a really fine landscape painter who is not also a fine draughtsman. And I think that inquiry will disclose the fact that the best of them have devoted at least four or five years pretty exclusively to the study of drawing. This is none too much. But the best place to acquire this knowledge, even for a landscape painter, is not out of doors before nature; because it is so much easier to study drawing indoors from the nude.

In art, as in the other affairs of life, those go fastest and furthest who follow the line of least resistance. In the open, therefore, our attention should be concentrated on the study of color, vibration, refraction, and the mystery of atmosphere – on those qualities in fact which can be studied nowhere else to the same advantage. But if a class of students in drawing should plant themselves down in the woods, using the oaks, the elms and the beeches for models, their progress toward an exact and synthetic knowledge of form would be slow indeed. The tree forms would permit them too much latitude. The articulation of a limb upon the trunk of an oak, for instance, might start a foot higher up or a foot lower down and still be in character, but the articulation of a knee joint, an elbow, or a shoulder of the human figure must be true to the inch. In fact, nowhere else can the sense of form be so perfectly trained as in following the exquisite and subtle lines of the most beautiful, the most perfect thing in nature – the nude human figure. Therefore, although we take it for granted that the drawing of a landscape shall be good, it is not in the drawing of landscape itself that landscape drawing can best be learned. When the eye is once trained to see and feel the infinite delicacies of the human form, it will find no difficulties in any of the other forms of nature. A landscapist should, of course, familiarize himself with the character of the trees, the hills, the turn of winding streams and of hillside roads by making frequent pencil drawings from nature, but he should first of all learn to draw.

Hence, when the student brings in badly drawn landscape studies, the only thing to do is to send him back to town; or, if he happens to be a capable draughtsman, erring through carelessness, to tell him to spend more time with the charcoal and less with the brush. It has been suggested that in order to keep the eye of the student always keyed up in drawing, it might be well to have a class in outdoor figure painting connected with every school of landscape art. This idea gained numerous adherents at the time of the wonderful exhibition in New York of the Spanish painter, Sorolla y Bastida. Nor was this to be wondered at; for these brilliant and exquisite studies of outdoor Spanish life, the figures throbbing with vitality, and the very air palpitating with the gay southern sunshine, might well excite the enthusiasm of all lovers of art; and their astounding realism, coupled as it was with a true sense of beauty, was the very thing that would be sure to fascinate the younger painters. Nevertheless nothing, in my opinion, could be less intelligent than the above suggestion. For the student who aims to go far in art the golden rule is, *one thing at a time*.

It you consider for a moment, you will perceive that painting the figure in the open involves a simultaneous attack on nearly every problem in the wide domain of art. You have first of all the outdoor questions of atmospheric vibration and refraction, and the consideration of the color-scale and value-scale; then, in addition to these, you have practically all the indoor problems, which include figure composition and arrangement, in addition to the usual problems of drawing and modelling – the latter presented in a reversed and unfamiliar form, owing to the new and unexpected color-reflections from the sky and the surrounding sunlit landscape. Of course, if this kind of study were regarded as merely a form of dissipation, a little spree as it were, to vary the dull monotony of landscape routine, it might have its good points. Change is a great tonic; and it does no harm occasionally to shoot arrows at the stars even if you know that they will not carry. But for students seriously to shoulder all these problems at once, shows both courage and naivete, but little discretion. Did they know that Sorolla himself worked for twenty-five years at the problem before he painted his first successful outdoor canvas, they would perhaps attack it with less enthusiasm. But courage is an admirable thing, and it seems a shame to put obstacles in its path.

I have said that Holbein and Leonardo da Vinci were probably two of the greatest draughtsmen the world has ever seen, stating at the same time that the character of their work precluded the possibility of really good painting as we moderns conceive it. Depending as it does for its distinction upon extreme delicacy and finesse of line, free and vibrant brushwork was of course not possible. There, fortunately, is another and larger manner of drawing which is peculiarly fitted for the true painter's use. This is drawing by mass, as it is seen in the work of J. F. Millet, Winslow Homer, and the French landscapist Harpignies. As landscape art in its highest expression is a synthetic grouping of masses of delicate and beautiful color, this kind of drawing is that which is made for the landscape painter's special needs. It allows full scope for the true rendering of character in all the principal forms, and at the same time it lends itself to the large and noble vision – for, even in drawing, the true *painter* must always see big. Here, as elsewhere, he must "grab the essential" and cast the little and the inessential behind him.

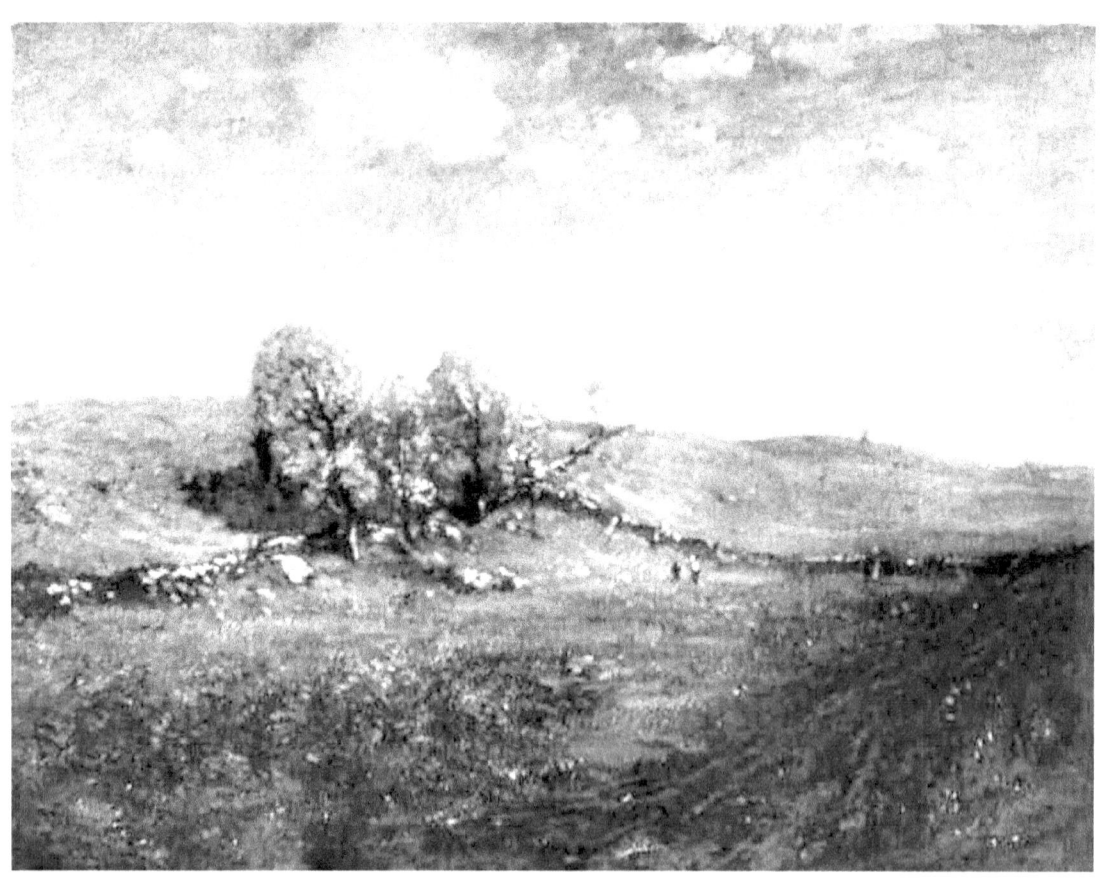

H. W. Ranger
Landscape

·VII·

Composition

There are so many millions of good compositions in the world that it seems strange anyone should ever waste time on a bad one. The good ones lie about us at every turn of the road. All that is necessary is the eye to see them. There are no fixed and immutable laws of composition – at least, none that cannot frequently be broken to advantage by a man of genius. All of the old conventional rules are explanatory rather than constructive. They may prevent an utterly bad arrangement, but they can hardly enable us to create a masterpiece; for the all-essential note of personality would be absent. In my own opinion, about all of the rules of composition which are of any practical value to a painter, are negative rather than positive, and can best be expressed in a series of "don'ts."

The first and by far the most important of these is, "don't try to say two things on one canvas." Any motive that is worth painting must have a central point of interest. Concentrate on that and sacrifice everything else to it. If there chance to be another attractive feature in the same subject, ruthlessly suppress it, in order that the one thing which you have to say may be said strongly. It often happens in nature that there are two points of nearly equal interest in the same scene. In this case divide the motive into two separate pictures, or else paint some other motive. If you try to paint both on the same canvas you will fall between two stools; for the human mind is capable of receiving but one impression at a time. An instance of this double motive which recurs constantly in nature is the scene where some handsome landscape is reflected in a pool or stream, the reflection being often more beautiful than the scene which it reflects. It would be fatal to attempt to reproduce both in one picture. The eye of the spectator would not know upon which of the two pictures to rest and neither would make its full impression.

An excellent example of the correct way to treat this motive is to be found in the river views of the Norwegian painter, Fritz Thaulow, who never gives more of the landscape itself than a suggestion at the top of the picture, thus concentrating the attention on the beautiful swirling expanse of water below. The water itself tells all that is needful of the thing it reflects, and the attention is not distracted in the effort to see two things at once.

I have seen many a poor picture in which two very excellent pictures had been painted upon the same canvas, either of which would have been beautiful by itself. If you wish your message to carry, don't confuse your audience with irrelevancies. Make your single statement clear and forceful and convincing – and let it stand by itself. Don't try to give too much for the money. This is even a worse mistake in art than it is in business.

Secondly. "Don't divide your picture into spaces of equal size and proportion." For some psychological reason of which we have not the explanation, the human mind abhors an equal division of space in a picture. Therefore don't put either your horizon line or your principal object of interest in the exact centre of the canvas. *How far* above or how far below, the centre the horizon should be placed, will of course depend upon the character of the motive and its various units. Unless there is some very convincing reason for the high horizon, however, all experience points to the lower division as best. A vast sky always lends nobility to a picture; while the suppression or nearly total elimination of the sky tends to convert the canvas into a sort of transcendent still-life. This is the case with the water pictures of Thaulow. They are the very apotheosis of still-life, it is true, but they are held within the still life class by the fact that they are a representation of nearby *objects*, that they make no appeal to the infinite – translate no mood or effect.

The low horizon line is peculiarly essential when the principal motive of the picture is found in the sky itself – some vast composition of rolling clouds, some gorgeous sunburst radiating its luminous streamers athwart the canvas, some castle in the air towering up and up to the zenith. In this case, a mere line of land is often sufficient – enough to give the dark and solid value that lends light and air to the upper reaches of the sky.

"Don't have anything in the picture which does not explain itself." Because a thing happens to exist in nature is no reason why it should be allowed a place in your picture – which is a work of art. Treat nature with respect and affection, but don't let her rule you. And, moreover, don't paint any motive that is so unusual and *outré* that it will not explain itself without a pamphlet attached to the frame. I once asked Mr. Lhermitte, the veteran French master, what he proposed to call an important picture which he had just then completed for the Salon. "I don't know," he replied. "A picture which needs a title should never have been painted. What would you call it yourself?" We had best not poach upon the preserves of the story-teller, because he can always beat us at his own game. No beauty was added to a certain picture of the Cornish coast which I once saw in the Royal Academy, by the fact that it was entitled "Where the Phoenicians came for tin."

"Don't repeat the main line of your picture with another important line parallel to it." If you have a mountain form swinging up to the left, have your clouds swing up to the right; or *tend* in that direction. If you are painting in a flat country like Holland, and your horizon line is forcedly horizontal, make this straight line beautiful by adjusting the cloud forms to it in agreeable contrast. The sky is in this respect a wonderful resource to the painter, for its lines may sweep in any one of an hundred different directions; and they can thus always be made to balance or accentuate or modify the lines of the solid earth, which cannot change.

Above all, "don't let the dominant line of your picture end aimlessly in mid-air." With the sky to help, there is no excuse for this. It should be picked up and carried on in a sinuous, living line, like the sweep of a winding brook or the curve of a mountain road.

The psychological effect of this living line in a picture is one of the most potent, though one of the most mysterious, things in art.

As I have already said, however, there is not one of these rules, nor one of the old conventional tenets, that cannot occasionally be disregarded to advantage. No! In this I am mistaken. There is one rule at least which must never be broken – the rule which says "thou shalt not paint two pictures upon one canvas;" for the house which is divided against itself inevitably falls to the ground.

But I have seen an excellent picture in which the horizon line bisected the canvas exactly in the centre – the necessary balance being achieved by other means. I have also seen pictures in which the repetition of the dominant line added a strange beauty to the canvas.

"Don't crowd your composition." Let your tree or your mountain have breathing space. Keep them away from the edge of the frame. They will gain in dignity and *apparent* bigness by diminishing rather than increasing their proportions.

"Don't put in a single unnecessary feature." Everything which does not contribute to the grace, or the beauty, or the force, or the sentiment of your picture detracts from it.

But unquestionably the best rule of all is to keep the eyes always wide open and observant of the things about you, for the most beautiful compositions in the world are always the daring and unexpected arrangements of nature. It behooves us to see them.

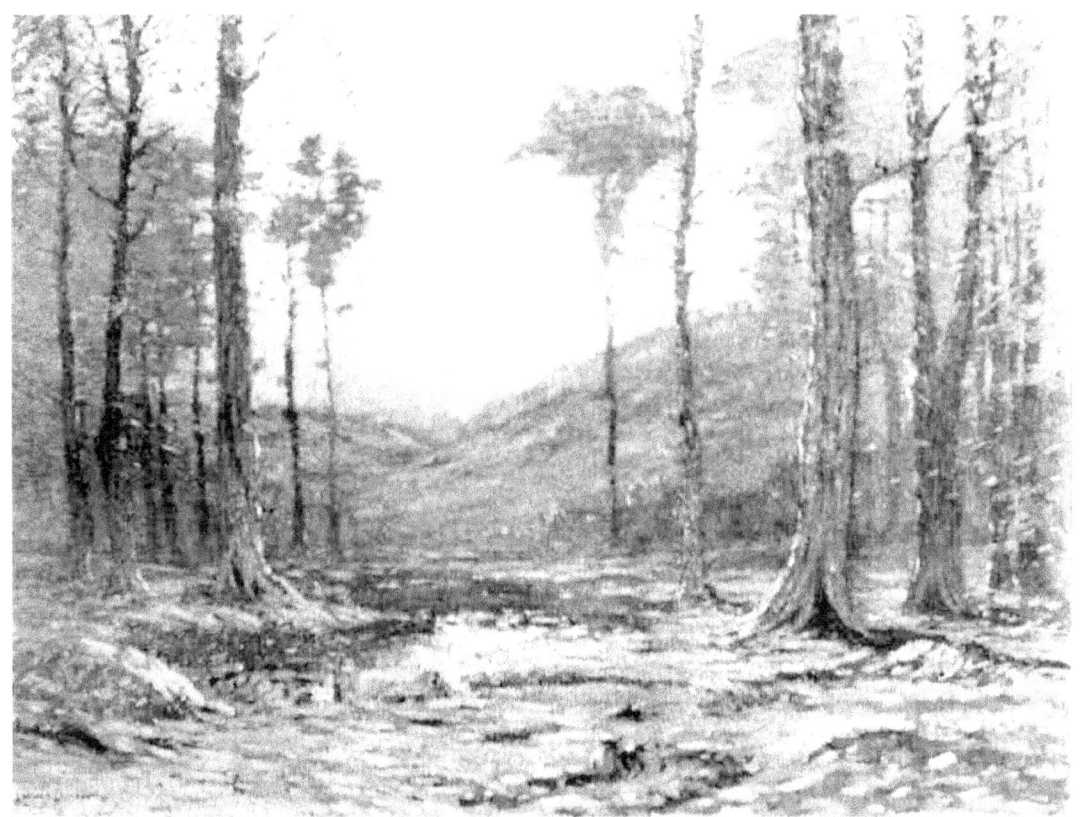

Leonard Ochtman
Wood Interior

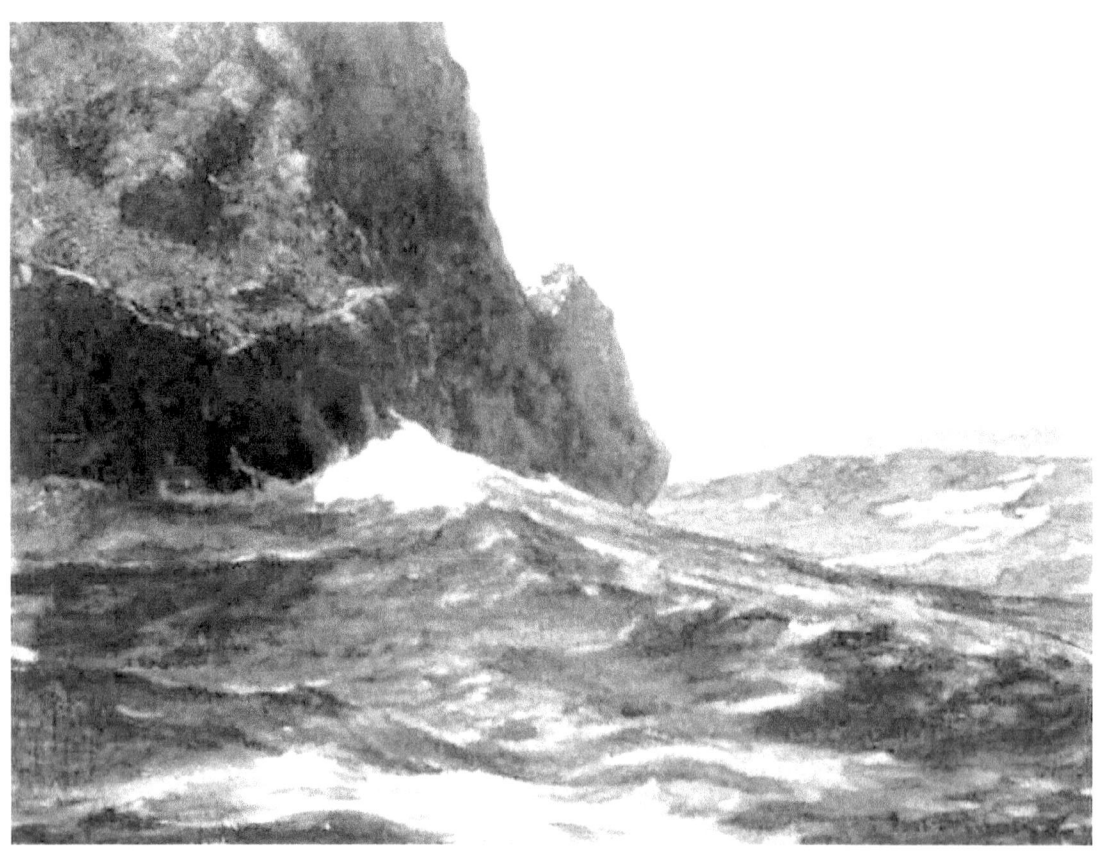

Paul Dougherty
Land and Sea

·VIII·

Quality

The Belgian master, Alfred Stevens, was wont to say that a picture in order to be truly great must excel from two different points of view. When seen from a distance it must be handsome in color, fine in composition, and true to the scene depicted; and when examined at close range the pigment must reveal that precious and jewel-like surface which is described by the word "quality."

Jean François Millet, on the contrary, abhorred quality, and vehemently protested that any painter who concerned himself with surface prettiness was little better than an artisan – at best a jeweler out of his element. Personally, I am inclined to think that both of these great masters were in the wrong, but that Millet came nearer to the truth than Stevens. It is quite certain, at any rate, that his instinct was correct in so far as it applied to his own work. Preciosity of surface could only detract from such a picture as the "Sower" or the "Shepherdess," while it would be a positive offence in a picture such as the "Man with a Hoe," Millet, of course, was too great and true an artist to fall into this error. His pictures give evidence of an infallible instinct for the eternal fitness of things, and as he was concerned always with *the thing to be said*, he used every resource at his command to reinforce the dominant idea of the work, suppressing every thing which might distract the attention from the central motive. The epic of labor was his message; and the coarse and often repellent surface texture of his pictures was in absolute harmony with the character of his subjects. These, while not precisely tragic, were invariably sober and serious, with the large dignity of primitive things.

But the fact that an enamel-like beauty of surface was not in keeping with the art of Millet is no valid proof that it has not a legitimate place of its own in painting. Indeed, the whole question of the relative value of things in art is here involved. The time is no longer when the figure painter can look down upon the landscape painter, when the painter of vast historical compositions has his special place reserved for him at the head of the board, while the painter of mere portraits must be content with a seat below the salt. It is the intrinsic beauty of the work itself that decides its value, and neither the size of the canvas nor the character of the subject counts. A portrait by Velasquez, a landscape by Corot, or a tiny still life by Chardin may very well be worth a dozen great figure compositions by

Le Brun or Van Loo. To withhold praise therefore from one of the bewilderingly beautiful pipe-dreams of Monticelli would be to deny the value of all the decorative art in the world; to say that the mere sensuous beauty of the flower or of the peacock's feather has no value because it delivers no intellectual message; to brush aside as worthless the ceramic art of Japan, the textiles of Persia, and the cathedral glass of the Middle Ages.

But just as we should deprecate the presence of a precious surface quality in one of Millet's noble and homely canvases, so we should resent any attempt at a didactic or serious message in a picture by Monticelli or Watteau. And herein lies the mistake of Alfred Stevens. Throughout all the ages the great masters have been content to say but one thing upon one canvas; to subordinate everything else in the picture to the one dominant idea, and to eliminate everything which does not contribute to reinforce it. As I have already said in the chapter on Composition, any attempt to convey two ideas at one and the same time leads to inevitable confusion. Each idea may be beautiful in itself, but the beauty of one will nullify the beauty of the other. Indeed, the fact that a secondary idea in a picture is especially interesting is the strongest argument for its suppression. If the idea is of sufficient beauty it deserves a canvas by itself, and should be reserved for another picture to be painted later on.

Of the works of Monticelli, Watteau, Gaston La Touche, and their fellows, we therefore ask no more than they have given us. We are content to saturate our souls in their sensuous loveliness; to take deep draughts of this intoxicating wine of beauty and to dream the day away. We do not say that their work is greater or less great than that of Millet or Winslow Homer or the other master painters of humanity. We only say that it is different, and we are glad that it is as it is and not otherwise. In the garden of art there are many mansions. We love to wander from one to another under the wide and bosky shade, and are happy that we must not dwell always in the same palace – be it ever so beautiful.

Now there is no question but that this elusive and exquisite surface beauty – this so-called "quality" – is peculiarly at home in some forms of landscape art. Of this we have indubitable proof in the work of Claude and Turner and in the pictures of our own painters, Ranger, Dearth, and Bunce. One thing, however, must not be lost sight of. When the picture is intended to deliver a message – to convey some poetic or strongly dramatic "mood" of nature, the unreserved use of quality may lead to the pitfall of the double motive. But when the character of the subject is quiet and idyllic, the sensitive appreciation of surface beauty on the part of the artist and his dexterous manipulation of pigment to secure it is not only legitimate but practically mandatory. Some of the most enduring works of beauty in painting owe their charm almost wholly to this one thing.

It is sometimes objected that there are various receipts by the use of which quality can be secured by the first comer. If this were true, it would be the greatest of boons to the artistic profession. But, alas! the only real receipt for quality is to be born a colorist. The kind which is secured by simple recourse to the varnish-pot is a sadly spurious article, which will bring little pleasure to anyone with a sensitive artistic organization. Quality which is obtained at the expense of truth is dearly bought, and varnish in itself does not make art.

When, therefore, I am asked by students for the best way to secure quality in a picture, I feel inclined to paraphrase the reply of Oliver Wendell Holmes to the reporter who asked him the best way to make sure of a long life. "The best way," said the Autocrat, "is to select long-lived parents."

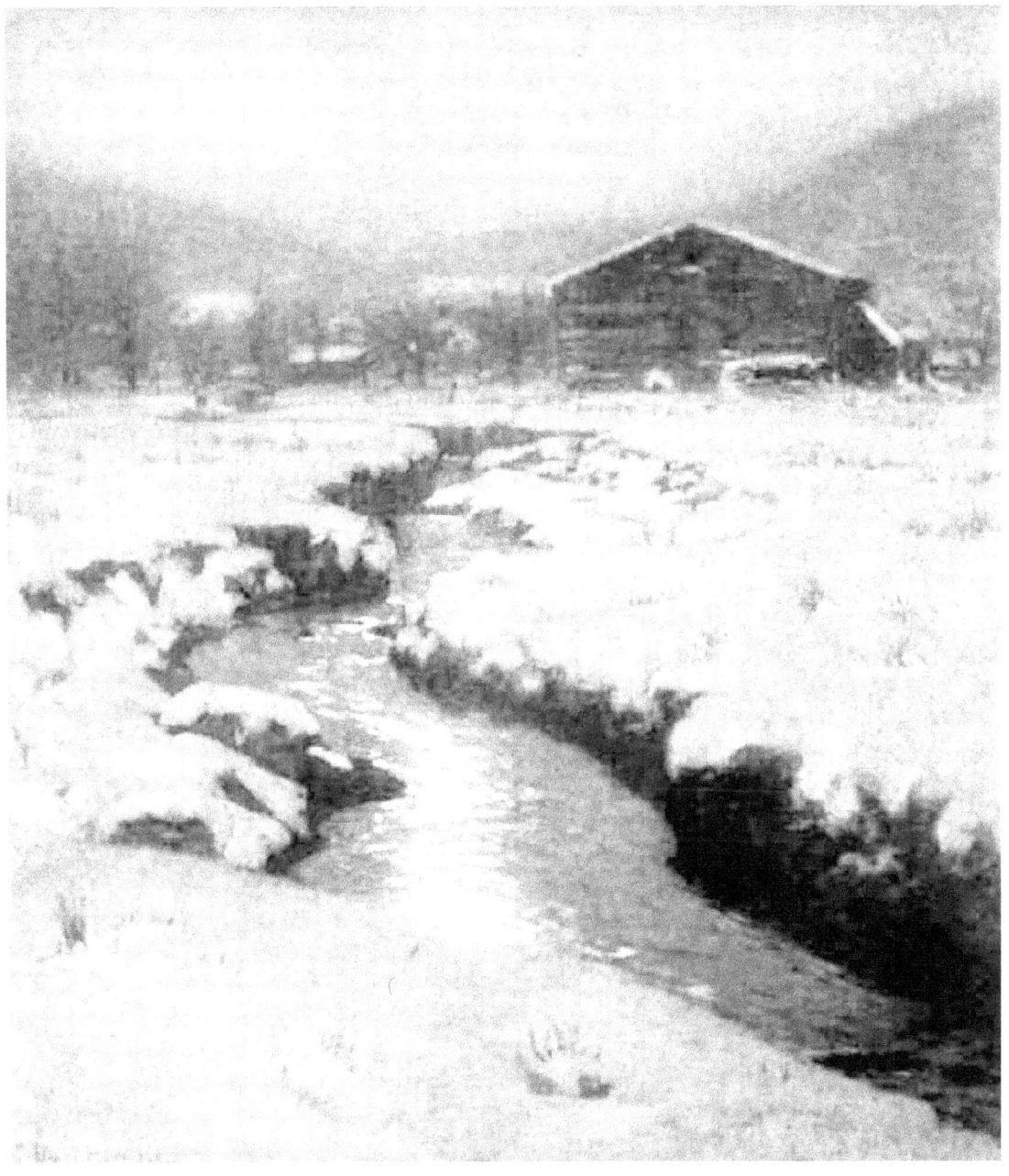

Birge Harrison
Woodstock Meadows in Winter

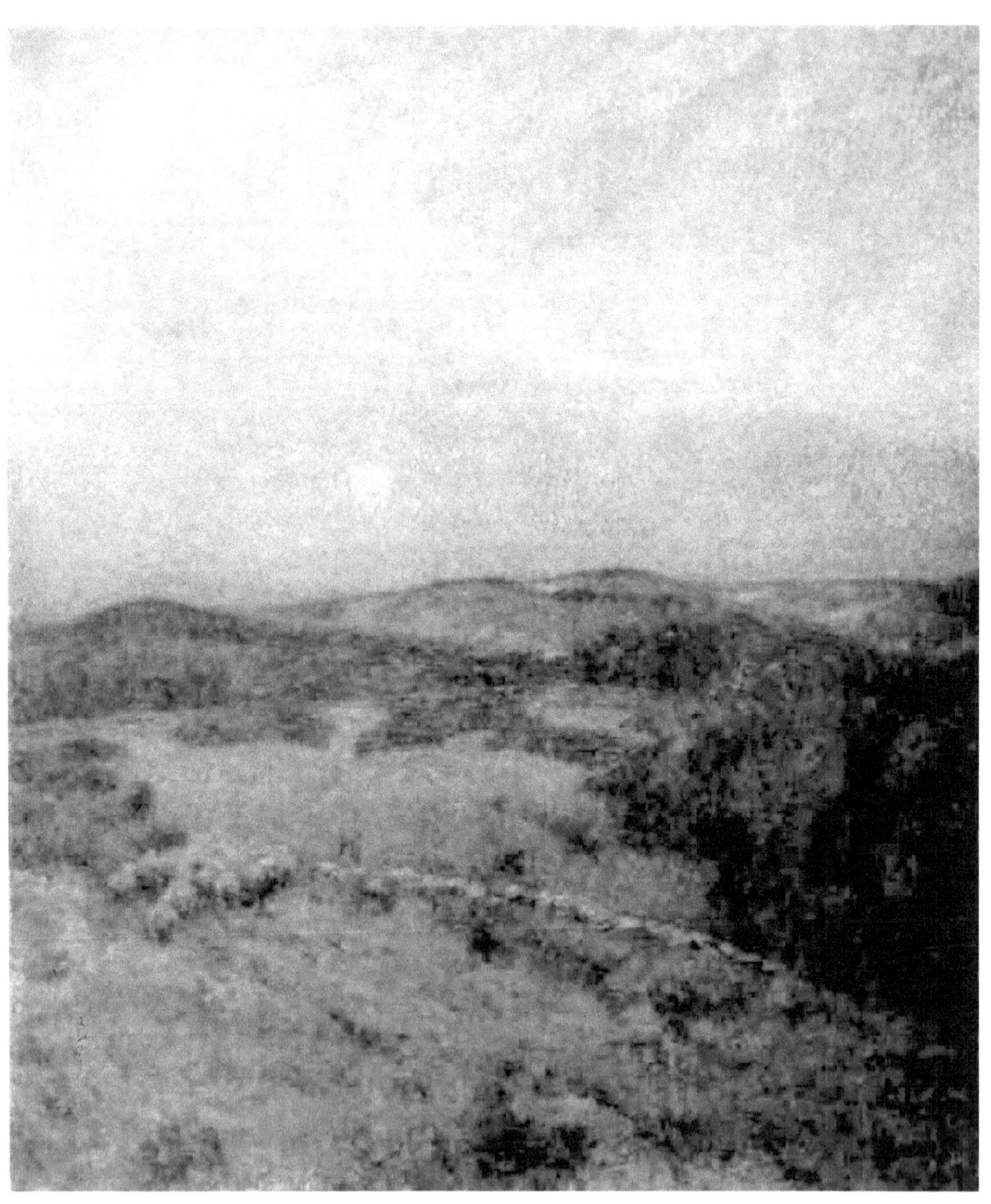

Ben Foster
Early Moonrise

·IX·

Pigments

The question of the medium in which the painter shall execute his pictures is an affair of temperament. Each artist must consult his own feelings in this matter and select the medium which is to him the most sympathetic. Today, there are practically but three systems of painting in common use, tempera having gone out of vogue, and fresco having very wisely been discarded in favor of better and sounder methods. The three remaining methods are, of course, pastel, watercolor, and oil. Each of these has its own special advantages, and its countervailing disadvantages.

Pastel, the most exquisite and fascinating of the three is also technically considered the most dangerous. It has, indeed, so many drawbacks on the material side that only the most thoroughly trained technician is able to avoid them all, and thus assure to his picture the permanence which is a first essential in any work of art. To begin with, it is the most fragile of materials. If a fixative is used it must be applied with a sure knowledge of the results to be obtained; for any carelessness or ignorance of manipulation during this delicate process will result in a certain loss of the surface bloom – the quality which more than anything else gives to pastels their exquisite charm. This statement applies more particularly to the painting in which the pastel is applied as a heavy coat over the whole surface of the canvas, and in which, therefore, fixing is an absolute necessity. When the pastel is used meagerly, and the surplus pigment is thoroughly shaken off, a pastel is nearly as indestructible as any other drawing, and this without the use of fixatives. But the worst shortcoming of pastel is its tendency to fade. This is unnecessary and is due solely to carelessness on the part of the manufacturers. The remedy, therefore, is to patronize only the most reliable makers.

Watercolor has many of the charms of pastel, with practically no demerits. Its permanence amply demonstrated by the cartoons of Raphael and Leonardo, while it gives to our work an airy delicacy that can be secured by no other means. Its only disadvantage is also one of its chief attractions – the element of uncertainty always present, for the color dries out a tone lighter than the freshly applied wash, and of course only long training enables one to discount with absolute certainty this subtle change of tone. However, we must admit that its usefulness is limited to comparatively light effects, and to pictures of moderate size, as it lacks the necessary depth and power for low-toned pictures or for canvases of large dimensions. As the lead factor is not present in watercolor work, almost the whole scale of pigments may be used with impunity and with reasonable certainty of permanence.

But of all the methods of painting yet discovered, painting in oil is unquestionably the most valuable and the most satisfactory in its general results, The range of its power is only limited to the power of the pigments at our command; and its permanence depends only on our care in the selection of these pigments. In this respect, however, it must be admitted that our palette is still far from ideal.

That in this age of chemical conquest we should still be using the sixteenth century colors; still be forced to pick and choose our pigments in the constant fear of chemical change, is a pointed comment on the intelligence of the artist fraternity. Had painters been able to combine in a united demand, they would long ago have had a palette as brilliant as the rainbow and as enduring as the pyramids. They ask no impossibility. Indeed, the solution of this problem would be a comparatively simple matter for the modern chemist, a mere nothing in comparison with the prodigies that have been wrought in the domain of steel and in the field of electricity. But alas! from the very nature of things, concerted action was impossible. The artist is a hopeless individualist. Were he able to sink his individuality in any merger, he would no longer be an artist. I have in mind a dinner given by a benevolent lover of art and artists, to which a dozen prominent painters were bidden, that they might explain their needs to an eminent chemist who was the guest of the evening. I shall not soon forget the bewilderment of the man of science at the end of the conference. In less than an hour he had received a dozen widely varying accounts of the needs of the profession, each one describing the special and individual needs of a special painter. Moreover, the discussion was so filled with gay and reckless persiflage, so shot through with wit and repartee, that it was hopeless to attempt to separate the light from the serious. It was a very gay party, but it advanced little the cause of sound color.

If, therefore, artists are ever to secure the pigments which they need, the demand must come from some alien source. Fortunately, this demand has already arisen. The manufacturers of print goods all over the world are insisting upon pigments which will remain permanent under the strong rays of the tropical sun, and which will at the same time resist the action of the various alkalies and acids they are sure to encounter in the wash-tub. To meet this demand one great firm of color makers has a hundred expert chemists employed upon the problem. Already they have achieved one definite and splendid result – a synthetic red which is absolutely neutral, chemically considered, and ten times more powerful than the best vermilion. As an artist's color, it replaces almost all the other red pigments which we have inherited from the past. The same chemists have an equally powerful yellow and blue under careful observation, and it is highly probable that in another year or two these, also, will be given to the world. Now it is evident that if painters can secure these three primary colors in two values, a light and a dark shade, they will, with the addition of white and black, have a perfect palette; as all of the secondary and tertiary colors, such as orange, green, violet, and their various derivatives can be compounded by an admixture of these original pigments.

But while we may *hope* for the completion of the new color-scale, it would be foolish prematurely to assume it as assured. In the meantime, we must act as if we were always to be dependent upon the old hereditary palette. That splendid and durable results can be secured through its use is amply proved by the superb examples of the old masters which have come down to us in a perfect state of preservation. All that is required is a little care and intelligence in the selection of the pigments. Lead is the one dangerous factor.* If we were willing to take from the palette the white lead and the chromes, which have also a lead basis, we could use almost all the other pigments with impunity. But our only substitute for white lead is zinc white, which has the disadvantage of being so extremely brittle when hard-dry, that it cracks when the canvas is rolled, or under the action of extremes of heat and cold.** The danger from lead is its strong affinity for sulphur, and the unfortunate fact that sulphide of lead is a blackish brown. Therefore when any of the colors containing sulphur (such as vermilion and the cadmiums) are mixed with either white lead or the chromes, we are sure to evolve the deadly sulphide, and there results a general browning or greening of the whole picture.

The rule, then, is either to content ourselves with zinc white, or, if white lead is used, to cast aside the cadmiums, vermilion, and emerald green (which, having a copper basis, is also subject to change when brought into contact with sulphur). The vermilion, fortunately, has now been replaced by the new color (which has been named by its makers Harrison red); and the cadmiums are hardly necessary, as they can be replaced by the chromes. Thus, with either lead white or zinc white, we have a very extended range, which has been greatly strengthened of late years by the addition of the two superb and perfectly safe alizarine colors, the scarlet and the crimson varieties. Neither the yellow nor the green alizarine can yet be claimed as perfectly sound and enduring; but then neither is essential.

Now, with this list of twenty or thirty pigments to select from, the question arises, naturally, as to the choice we shall make from them; for it is evident, I think, that even the most courageous amateur would hardly venture upon the whole gamut at one time. In the first place, it may be said that choice of palette is a matter of temperament. Each student must experiment with the various pigments and select those which he personally finds most sympathetic. But, in general, it is best to eliminate all the secondary or compound colors, such as green, purple, etc.; and this for two reasons: first, because a painter secures more vibration in his work by mixing his own secondary and tertiary tones; and, second, because if one has a green on the palette, one is very apt to use that special green, instead

*Editor's note: The mixture of lead white with vermilion or cadmium colors is not the cause of discoloration in an oil painting. Improperly prepared vermilion, containing traces of chloride, can react with light which results in the appearance of black spots on the painting. Properly made vermilion does not contain chloride and therefore will not darken any more appreciably than other colors. See, http://www.sciencedaily.com/releases/2005/07/050708060730.htm

**Zinc white has been proven to crack. "Paints made with zinc oxide and drying oils become extremely brittle in as little as three years. Paints containing zinc oxide exhibit severe delaminating problems after drying and this is especially true of zinc oxide paint on acrylic emulsion grounds. Even commercial lead white and titanium white oil paints containing zinc oxide become quite brittle after seven years of drying." -George O'Hanlon, Technical Director, Natural Pigments (naturalpigments.com) of searching out the various greens (and they are infinite) that may enter into his picture motive. It may also be stated as an axiom, that the more experienced the artist, the more limited is his palette. The expert cannot be bothered with useless pigments. He selects the few that are really essential and throws aside the rest as useless lumber. The distinguished Swedish artist, Zorn, uses but two colors – vermilion and yellow ochre; his two other pigments, black and white, being the negation of color.* With this palette, simple to the point of poverty, he nevertheless finds it possible to paint an immense variety of landscape and figure subjects, and I have never heard his color criticized as being anemic or lacking in power. Many other painters limit themselves to five colors; and when the palette is extended beyond seven, it is safe to presume that one is skirting the borders either of the amateur or the student class.

So much for pigments. But now we are confronted with another and a still more difficult problem: that of the medium in which the colors are to be mixed. For this purpose nothing better than pure linseed oil has ever been discovered, and indeed nothing better could be desired; for it combines nearly all of the good qualities – transparency, hardness, a certain flexibility when dry, and a durability whose limits we are as yet unable to gauge – the first pictures ever painted in oil colors being still in a good state of preservation. Unfortunately it has now become very difficult to obtain pure linseed oil. Most of the oil of the world is at present extracted by the oil trust, which, in order to secure a slightly increased output, subjects the seed under pressure to a high heat, with the result that in addition to the oil there is pressed out of the mash a variety of resins and essential oils, whose ultimate chemical effect on our colors we cannot as yet determine. Finally, the whole output is boiled with a certain addition of litharge to help its drying quality, and litharge is *red lead*. So here the lead equation enters into our palette again, in spite of our best efforts to exclude it. There are, however, I believe, two color-men in the world who, recognizing the necessity of pure *raw oil* for artist's use, have recently established plants of their own, where the seed is pressed *cold* and the oil is left *raw*. These firms are Bloch and Winsor & Newton. There may, of course, be others of which I do not know. To ensure entire safety and durability, *nothing* but pure linseed oil should be mixed with the colors; all cracking, gumming, etc., being due to inequalities in the drying period of the different mediums used on our canvas. If anything at all is mixed with the oil, the safest and best thing in the world is certainly pure Venice turpentine. If kerosene is used, it should be carefully washed to eliminate all of the acid which is used in refining the crude oil. Otherwise this free acid will attack the lead and discolor it.

In regard to varnishing, the important thing is to allow the picture to dry thoroughly before the varnish is applied. Six months is none too much for this, and a year is far better. A picture varnished before the oil is hard-dry is certain to crack sooner or later, as the oil and the varnish dry at different rates of speed. The pictures of Rubens and Vandyke were varnished with a medium made by exposing pure linseed oil to the sunlight until it was quite thick. This required a month or two to dry thoroughly after it was applied to the picture; but the splendid preservation and the great brilliancy of Rubens's pictures have justified all the extra pains and trouble incident to the method which he employed.

*Editor's note: Zorn did in fact use more colors than Harrison suggests.

·X·

On Framing Pictures

A picture is a convention – an illusion. We take a few crude materials, a square of canvas, some earthy pigments, and by a sort of artistic legerdemain we propose to make those materials disappear and to persuade the spectator that he is looking *through* the frame and out over the sunny landscape beyond. If the magician is clever enough, if he observes carefully the laws of color, of values, and of refraction, he may succeed fairly well. But the slightest thing will break the spell. A scratch across the sky, a little indentation, and the illusion disappears; for the observer has become conscious of the *surface* of the canvas. The rough edge of the stretcher has the same disillusioning effect, and for this reason no picture is really complete until it is enclosed within the sheltering protection of a frame. It is necessary to separate the real from the unreal, the hard reality of the background of burlap or of wall-paper from the illusion of the picture.

Now the question at once arises as to the best form for this protecting barrier, the best material to use in its construction, and the best and most harmonious surface for its finish. Artists are all aware of the vital importance of this matter. They know that a frame can either make or mar their picture, and they give the subject constant thought and attention. At one period I devoted considerable time and study to the question and made voyages of discovery into many strange and untried fields.

Of course I tried frames of carved wood of various hues and varied design; I collected seashells and fishnets, poppy-stalks, ears of grain, and all sorts of beautiful dried weeds out of the fields, which I glued to the flat surface of my frames, and gilded. I made experiments also with textile fabrics applied between narrow bands of gold. At one time I cut up a superb Turkish rug and made me a precious frame of this exquisite material. Barbarous vandalism, if you will, but all in the good cause of art. However, that was the most disastrous frame of all. The rug was so beautiful that the unfortunate picture was entirely annihilated. The surface texture of the rug was in itself so compelling that no picture could stand up against it. It was this frame, however, which first showed me that I was on the wrong track. All of my shells and nets and weeds, although gilded, were *actual* objects, with which the eye was familiar. The observer as a consequence saw the *frame* when it was essential that he should see only the picture. The frame, I perceived at last, must be something midway between the real and the unreal – conventional in form and intangible in surface. And I rediscovered the fact, which the old masters had discovered so many centuries ago, that there was no material in the whole range of nature so admirably filled for the surface of a frame as gold or metal leaf. Next to the mirror, it presents the most elusive of all surfaces. Semi-reflecting, semi-solid, it is just the thing that fills all the requirements. So I came back home again and spent the rest of my time in a study of the best forms and the best tones of metal leaf to be employed. Fortunately, there is a large range of colors at our disposal, beginning with pure silver, and going through various tints of green, yellow, and orange gold to the deep red of copper – a gamut as extended as the most demanding painter could ask.

Here it soon became apparent that the law of complementaries reigned supreme. A picture whose dominant note was pink demanded a greenish gold frame, a blue picture called for a tone of pure yellow or orange gold, while a picture whose dominant tone was golden yellow could only be well clothed in silver. Fortunately, the dominant note of most landscapes is found in the blue or blue-gray sky, and thus the pure gold frame is its ideal casing. But there are pictures – often enchanting effects – which are killed by the juxtaposition of yellow gold; and these pictures are barred out of our exhibitions by the barbaric rule which limits *all* frames to those of gold leaf. One of my own most successful canvases, representing the interior of a birch wood in autumn, was a solid mass of shimmering yellow foliage, relieved only by the silvery notes of the slender and graceful trees. I tried it, without success, in every possible tone of gold leaf; but finally *had* to come to silver. The picture, of course, was "returned with thanks on account of the frame"; but it found an immediate purchaser in the first private exhibition at which it was seen. The price, moreover, had been doubled as a balm to my wounded feelings.

When it comes to the form and design of a frame, infinite latitude is allowable, but, in general, the law of contrast holds good here also. A very complicated picture which depends for its effect largely upon some graceful and intricate design will show to best advantage in a comparatively flat and simple frame. A simple picture, on the contrary, which is built up with a few broad and powerful masses, will frequently appear best in a rich and ornamental frame, the very richness of design accentuating the simple beauty of the canvas. If, however, the value-scale of a picture is extremely delicate, this must also be taken into account, and the frame, though ornamental in design, should be in low relief, in order to harmonize with the picture which it is to frame. The question of the mat surface and the burnished surface, or the proportion of each to be allowed in a given frame, must depend upon the special picture under consideration, and also upon the individual taste of the painter. The worst frame of all, the only inexcusable one, is the blatant, vulgar over-ornate, over-wide, over-burnished affair, which cries out, "look at me, I cost five hundred dollars, so this picture must be worth five thousand."

·XI·

On Schools

If the infant Sargent or Whistler had been marooned with a savage tribe and brought up beyond the furthest confines of civilization, what would their art have amounted to? We may presume that they would have carved the totem pole just a little more cleverly than their savage mates, or have given the idol's features a twist more of deviltry or of intelligence. But this would have been the limit of their performance, for art is the child of time and of precedent. It inherits the ages; but unless the artist comes into his inheritance, he is helpless. At best, can he go but one little step beyond the fathers, add one little stone to the edifice; and in order to accomplish even this much, he must know well the work of his predecessors. If by some dreadful catastrophe all the art of the world should suddenly be destroyed and all knowledge of it blotted from the minds of the survivors, it would require ten thousand years for humanity to recover the lost ground. As an artist is dependent upon the past, it is evident that he must strive to see and to study all of the past art that he can find – to feed his mind constantly upon it. In the old days when the painter was a craftsman – a little higher than the workers in iron or in brass, in wood, or in the precious metals, but still in the same category – it was customary to apprentice lads to some well-known master. Velasquez was thus apprenticed at the age of thirteen, Perugino at nine, and Andrea del Sarto at the tender age of seven. Constantly under the master's eye, they learned their craft much as a tailor's apprentice learns his trade. When they were not grinding colors or stretching canvas, or sweeping out the studio, they were allowed to copy the master's work or possibly to fill in backgrounds for him, and they received his instruction in return for their labors. We do not hear of anything resembling the modern art school until the time of the brothers Carraci; and it thus happens that the graduates of the first genuine school of art were the painters of the Italian Decadence. There would seem to be a sinister significance in this coincidence – a significance which has been a facile argument in the hands of those who hold that schools of art exert a pernicious influence upon the student, destroying his individuality and his personal outlook. They forget that the effect of the school atmosphere is a bagatelle in comparison to the overwhelming influence of the private master, whose dominant personality must have been felt at every hour of the day for years at a stretch. The truth is that where an artist is born with the three essentials – temperament, character, and sincerity – it is *impossible* to destroy the personal note in him. Nothing can submerge it. The main thing is for him to acquire knowledge and more knowledge and still more knowledge, and the source of his information matters not one whit.

Personally, I am convinced that the synchronous arrival of the art school and the Decadence of Italian art was a mere coincidence, and that the modern system of art instruction – the great art school with its corps of instructors – is a distinct improvement over the ancient method. It will be readily seen and understood, for instance, that, unless a master chances to be exceptionally intelligent, he will be apt to insist upon the student's using his own palette and his own technical methods, and this will delay the acquisition of the personal color-scale and the personal technic most fitted to the individual needs of each different student. This can be, and often is, corrected by the outside study and investigations of students themselves, but it were better that the influence had never been exerted.

On the whole it may be said that our great schools both here and abroad are singularly free from this defect, and that they give to the really serious student ample facility for a thorough training in drawing, painting, composition, and all the fundamentals of art as understood by the great masters of other times. The schools, however, have in some respects not kept pace with the progress of modern art, and the student graduating from the class has still many things to learn for and by himself before he can put into his work the qualities which distinguish the art of our own times from that of the past. My own experience of twenty-five years ago is still very generally the experience of students leaving the schools today.

I left the École des Beaux Arts, after six years of hard and conscientious labor, and drifted down to Brittany, fully prepared, as I believed, to paint medal pictures for the Salon.

I gathered together a collection of stunning subjects, laid them in bravely, and set to work to develop them into pictures, according to the rules and standards which I had learned in Paris. I confess that I was somewhat surprised when, at the end of a year's work, I had not a single satisfactory canvas to show. At the end of eighteen months I began to suspect that something was radically wrong, and when, at the end of two years, I was still without a picture worthy of the name, I became genuinely discouraged.

About this time I was at work on another huge "Salon," a canvas some twelve by eight feet in dimension, if I remember rightly, which depicted the interior of a birchwood in autumn, with a single figure of a peasant girl raking up the dead leaves. The work was well toward completion. It was, I knew, well drawn, sound in values, and at least as true and delicate in color as the average picture. It was an honest endeavor, at any rate, and my very best; yet down deep in my heart I felt that it was a failure, like all the others. But the heartbreaking part of it was that I could not guess *why* it was a failure.

One day, as I was painting away conscientiously, a friend strolled by – a Scandinavian painter for whose work I had the most profound admiration. After studying my effort for awhile he remarked:

"Harrison, that thing of yours is so good it is a pity it is not a d----d sight better."

"Well, for Heaven's sake, U.," I said, "tell me what is the matter with it."

"I am not sure that I could *tell* you," he replied, "but if you will lend me your palette for ten minutes I might, perhaps, be able to *show* you."

He selected an area of eighteen inches in the left centre of my composition, and in fifteen minutes had entirely repainted it. His work, as I studied it, did not vary in color, in tone, or in value from the surrounding portions of the picture which I had painted myself; yet it was as if a window had been opened in the centre of the canvas. U.'s work vibrated and sparkled with light and with atmosphere, while mine lay flat and dead. It was also as if a window had been opened in my own soul. U. had shown me the secret of atmospheric painting – had made clear to me in a single lucid demonstration the importance of vibration and refraction in landscape painting. I threw aside the canvas upon which I was at work and started another, which I carried through with such enthusiasm and verve as I can never remember having put into another work – using, of course, the new knowledge which had come to me so opportunely.

This picture really went to the Salon. It was hung upon the line, received a medal, and was bought by the French government for one of the national museums, where, doubtless, it still hangs.

I then and there made up my mind that if it ever came my turn to instruct young students I should endeavor to teach them those things for which we painters of the older generation had to grope blindly for years, unaided and in the dark – things which are of equal value and importance in a picture with good drawing, good composition, and good color, but which, for some reason, have never been taught in the regular art schools.

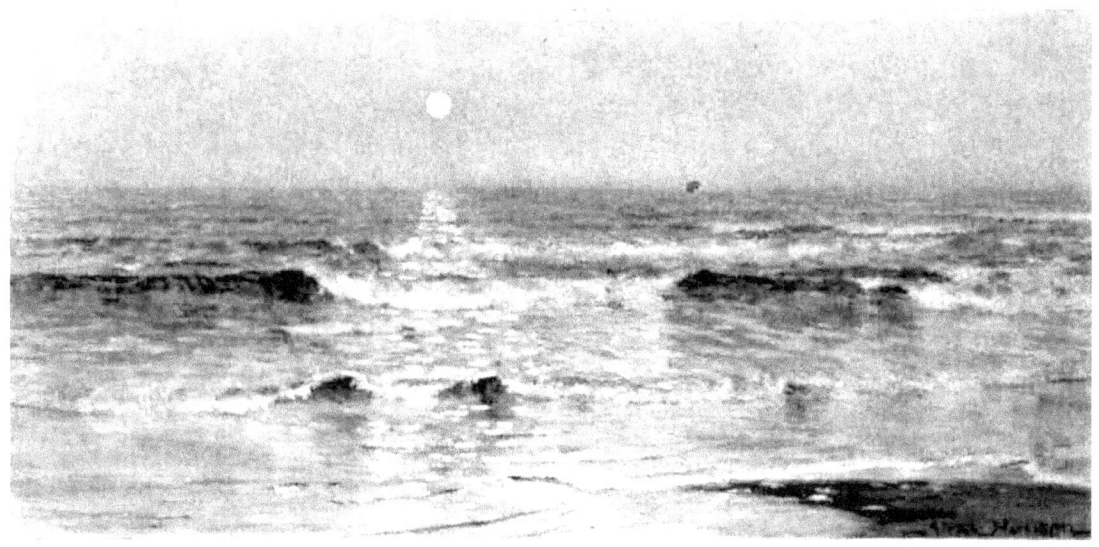

Alexander Harrison (Birge Harrison's brother)
La Crépuscule

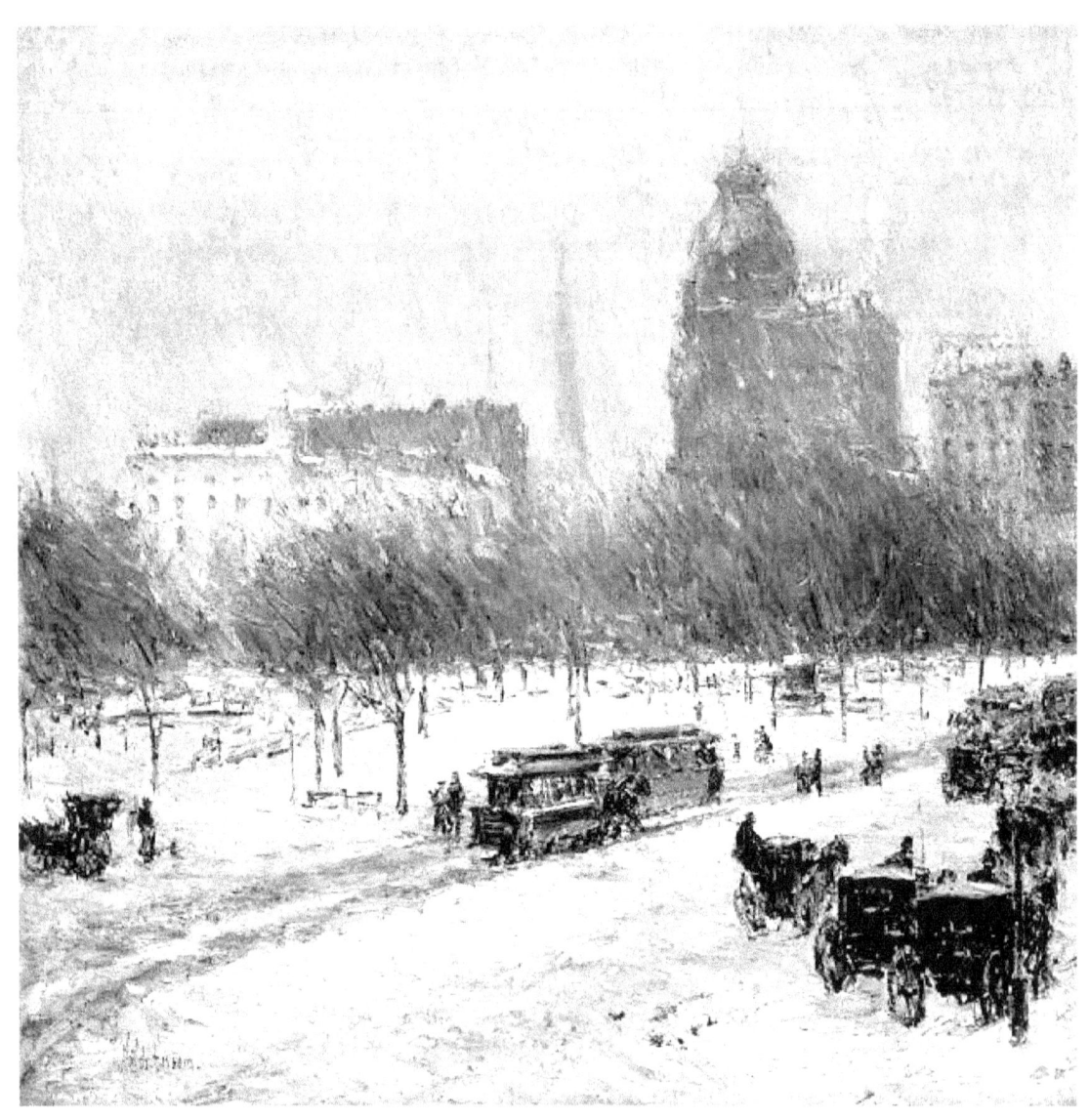

Childe Hassam
Union Square

·XII·

The Arts and Crafts

The "Free Art League of America" has recently printed an open letter, in which it congratulates the American people on the triumph of free art and rejoices over the certitude that valuable collections of old masterpieces will soon be brought to this country, and that beautiful carvings, bronzes, ivories, and antiques of all descriptions will drift into our museums, and into private collections all over the country. It finds particular satisfaction in the fact that these objects will now be at the service of our manufacturers for use as models, and that as a natural consequence "all of our manufactured products in which design plays an important part will be better able to compete with those of Europe."

We may indeed rejoice if we are at last to come into our heritage – so long withheld; if we may hope soon to secure our fair share of the treasures of the world. But if our only use for them is to copy them, to use them for models, it were better they should remain across the water. It is certain, I think, that America will one day have a school of decorative art that will win the universal admiration of the world; but if this is ever to happen, it will be because she has developed an art that is wholly her own; an art that is purely American; an art whose symbols will be the American flora and fauna as seen by American eyes and felt through the American temperament.

There is only one path by which an individual or a nation can hope to attain to eminence in art, or even in the "arts and crafts" – and that path always leads direct to nature. We may study the antiques, and joy in them, and fill our souls with their beauty, but for our inspiration we must ever hark back to nature and get as near her heart as ever we can. She has a special message of beauty for every sincere questioner, and the message she gives to me will differ from that which she holds for you, and the message she delivers to the Dutchman will not be the same as that which she gives to the Spaniard.

The decorative art of the Japanese is nature as the Japanese see it; the decorative art of the Hindus is nature as that strangely subtle and occult people see it; the decorative art of the Moors was nature as the Saracens saw it; and the decorative art of America must be nature as the Americans see it. There is no art so synthetic, so conventional, that it does not derive from nature, and the difference between the art of Persia and the art of Europe is the mental and temperamental difference between the Persian and the European. This is the foundation and explanation of all art, whatever period it represents, or from whatever country it emanates, and it applies with equal force to the decoration on a porcelain jug or to the greatest mural painting in the world.

Sincerity! Sincerity! That is the key to it all.

Of course it was comparatively easy for the Hindu or the Japanese or the Persian to be sincere and naive because the arts of other countries were unknown to them. But our wider knowledge is no handicap, no disadvantage to us if we only preserve our own integrity.

This we must do in absolute sincerity and without any mental reservation. Even in the development of the conventional forms, which are the basis of all decorative art, we cannot with safety use the rules which were invented and tabulated by the older craftsmen. We must invent our own systems. Having analyzed our bird or our leaf or our flower, we must select as the groundwork of our conventional design the particular form or tint that appeals to us as the most beautiful or the most graceful or fitting; and just because we are Americans, just because of the mental difference between ourselves and the men of other nations, our selection would be different from the selection made from the same basic elements by a Japanese, a Persian, or a Hindu, or a Frenchman, an Englishman, or a German; and in this slight difference at the beginning of things lies the germ of all that is distinctive and characteristic, and therefore of all that is truly beautiful in art.

·XIII·

Mural Painting

Mural painting occupies a position alone and by itself, midway between the purely conventional decoration and the realistic easel picture. It must be sufficiently real to tell its story; it must not be so real as to destroy the flatness and solidity of the surface upon which it is painted. Mural painting, in fact, must be considered as an adjunct of architecture, and not as a self-dependent creation. First of all, therefore, it must be in harmony with the architectural scheme of the room which it is supposed to decorate and adorn. It must not blatantly insist upon recognition, but must rather modestly invite the attention of the gaze which has at first been occupied with the proportions of the apartment, the hall, or the church which it helps to beautify. It is, in fact, applied art in the highest sense of the term. As a mural painting must always remain in its original position, it is peculiarly dependent upon its surroundings, and the mural painter has not only to consider the form and position of the space which the picture is to fill, but the color of the surrounding walls and the quantity and quality and direction of the light which it will receive. In its most important aspect, therefore, it is the exact opposite of the easel picture; for while the easel picture must, first of all, be true to nature and express nature's mood, the mural decoration must, first of all, be true to the architecture and express its mood. It must, in other words, pick up the scheme where the architect dropped it, and carry the same motive to still greater heights of beauty. Its *first* and most important function, therefore, is purely decorative, to fill and satisfy the eye with a surface of graceful line and sensuous and beautiful color. And the mural decorator who forgets this cardinal fact or is temperamentally incapable of working within the prescribed limits, should devote himself to some other line of art. It will be seen, therefore, that the rigid and enforced conditions under which the mural painter works impose upon him great reserve in his scale of color and of values. If he were to use the full scale of either (or anything approaching it), he would inevitably produce the *illusion* of the easel picture, which it is essential to avoid. His wall surface would apparently disappear, and one of the chief architectural unities would be violated. For the same reason a carved or gilded frame is not allowable on any purely mural decoration, the gold frame having been replaced by universal consent with a decorative border painted upon the flat surface of the wall, thus helping rather than hindering the sense of support and solidity that must be maintained at all costs. It is probable that the more the artist is willing to limit his scale of color, the more conventional he makes it, the more beautiful will be his result; and it is quite permissible to doubt whether any of the modem highly colored decorations have filled the first essential of mural art so well as the old-time tapestry with its limited scale of gray greens, gray blues, buffs, and yellows. It is quite certain at any rate that when Puvis de Chavannes in his decorations at the Sorbonne and the Pantheon cut the color-scale and the value-scale in half, we were all conscious of an unaccustomed and quite peculiar fitness of the means to the end; of a truth that was higher than the truth of nature, because it was the truth of art.

But although the color-scale of a mural painting may be limited or attenuated, it must still remain true within its limits. Even the tapestry is true *so far as it goes*. The human eye would repudiate scarlet grass or a grass-green sky. The elements of the decoration must come from nature exactly as they do in the easel picture, the difference being that in the latter case the painter accepts and utilizes practically *all* that nature gives him, while the mural painter takes from nature only those elements which will best subserve his ends.

It would, however, be absurd to assert that because the convention of the Gobelins, the Beauvais, and the Arras was beautiful and soul-satisfying, it must necessarily be the *ultima thule* of decorative art. It was simply one good form out of hundreds, many of which are yet to be discovered. The color schemes that could be utilized for this purpose are simply unlimited in number, and when the demand arises it is almost certain that another convention equally beautiful, though different, will appear right here in our own country. The new conditions of life in this new civilization make it impossible that our American scheme of decoration, when it is finally evolved, should be the same as that which grew out of the life and the conditions of medieval Europe.

Those of our artists who are foolishly occupied in copying or transposing the beautiful art of the ancients have entered a blind alley which ends against a blank wall. Imitation is the sincerest form of flattery, but in art it leads only to a fall.

Until very recent years, almost all important mural decorations were figure compositions in which landscape played only a minor part; but the trend of modern life points clearly to a time – a time in the very near future, I believe – when pure landscape will be largely used in mural work. We can already point to several important and eminently successful attempts of this kind in the city of New York, and there is little reason to doubt that this number will be added to rapidly as the fitness of the material for the purpose is recognized and the beauty and decorative quality of the result is seen and appreciated.

·XIV·

On Vision

Vision! the key to the door of art; the power to see with the eyes of the soul! as necessary to the artist as faith to the true believer. We have been talking of color, vibration, refraction, drawing, and so on – all so much useless lumber if a painter have not the one divine gift. I once knew an artist who had all these technical things at his finger tips; he was an able draughtsman, a strong colorist, and the difficulties of refraction and vibration were to him a mere bagatelle. Yet one of his pictures was like a man without a soul – a veritable Frankenstein Monster of art – for he lacked the artist vision.

Fortunately, the true vision is not a rare endowment. By the grace of God many of us are born with the sense of beauty; and even if we are gifted with but a tiny spark, this spark can be fostered until it grows into a clear and luminous flame whose light will transform the most commonplace scene or object into a vision of infinite loveliness. If we look always for beauty we shall come at last to find it in the most unexpected places and under many strange garbs. But the true vision means not only the power to see and to recognize beauty, but the power to see it stripped of all vulgarities and inessentials; the power to see the soul of the thing and to grasp its *essential* beauty. For any landscape has a soul as well as a body. Its body is our great rock-ribbed mother-earth with her endless expanse of fields and hills, of rivers and surging seas. Its soul is the spirit of light – of sunlight, of moonlight, of starlight – which plays ceaselessly across the face of the landscape, veiling it at night in mystery and shadow, painting it at dawn with the colors of the pearl-shell, and bathing it at midday in a luminous glory. To this and to the ambient and all enveloping atmosphere, with its clouds and its mists, its rain and its veiling haze, are due the infinite and ever shifting *moods* of nature. He who paints the body alone may be an excellent craftsman, but the true artist is he who paints the beautiful body informed and irradiated by the still more lovely and fascinating spirit – he who renders the *mood*.

The painter who lacks this greatest of all gifts, or who, having it, fails to use it, might just as well scrape his palette and close his color-box, for his message to humanity will not be worth the telling.

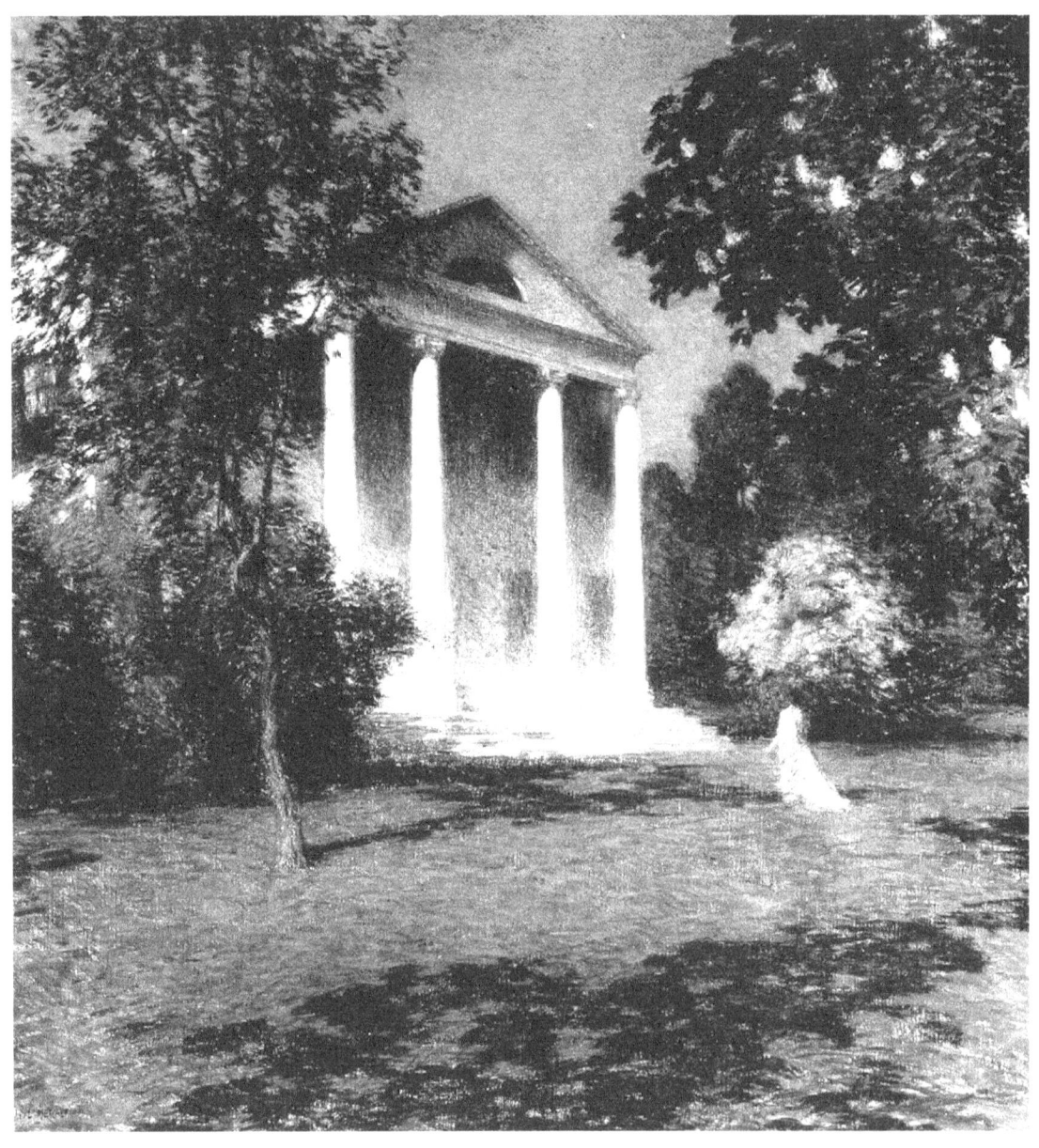

Willard Metcalf
Summer Moonlight

·XV·

The Importance of Fearlessness in Painting

Be courageous. Always dare to the limit of your knowledge and just a little beyond. You must show conviction yourself, if you would convince others. One of our best painters recently assured me that cheek was his only technical asset. This was not true, but it was half true.

The public loves to be dictated to in matters of art – to feel that the painter is "onto his job." It will pass by the man who says "I think," and stand rapt every time before the picture of the man who says "I know." Aim to tell the truth; but if you have to lie, lie courageously. A courageous lie has often more virtue than a timid truth. My brother, the marine painter, was once asked by a mutual friend to criticise two marines upon which the latter was at work. He went without enthusiasm, for the man had never attempted a sea-piece in his life – and it takes years to understand the ocean. On his return, I asked about it. "Why it was simply astounding," was the reply. "They were false of course. But they were so cheeky that they would convince anyone but a marine painter." When you know that this man was color-blind, and that he had compassed success in spite of his handicap, you will understand the kind of courage he dealt in.

Use plenty of pigment also – great "gobs" of it. A well-furnished palette is half the battle. Squeeze out twice as much color as you think you can possibly need, and then use it all. Look at the work of our friends Redfield, Sorolla, Foster, Schofield, Dougherty, Dearth, Chase – all the good *painters*. It shows clearly that they have plenty of paint upon their palettes. Never count the cost of your pigments. Use them as if they were the very dirt under your feet. There are difficulties enough in art without adding another to the list. At best (or worst) you can hardly use more than twenty dollars' worth of pigment on any one canvas, and that is a bagatelle in comparison to the thousands which you propose to ask for your picture. Paint with house paints if you are too poor to have a generous supply of the tube variety, but for Heaven's sake, don't stint your palette.

When I was working in France, some twenty years ago, one of the younger painters asked me for a criticism on his "Salon." I found him at work upon quite a large canvas, using a palette which was dotted with mere pin-points of color. The picture was well arranged and well "seen," but with *that* palette of course good painting was impossible. Carroll was a poor man. We were all aware that his allowance was barely sufficient to pay for the simplest of food and lodging; and the cost of artist's materials must have been a serious drain upon his slender resources. So I hesitated long before asking for his color box. There was but one thing to do, however; so, resolutely smothering all compunctions, I seized upon the precious tube of madder and squeezed out a most generous supply. Carroll jumped nearly out of his boots.

Good gracious!" he exclaimed, "why that amount would last me two weeks at least."

My only reply was to follow suit with the cobalt, the cadmium, and the ultramarine. In less than two minutes I had a palette as generously furnished as the most extravagant impressionist could desire.

"There, Carroll," I said, "that is the best criticism I can possibly give you. Use all those pigments this morning, and the result will be such a piece of painting as you have never done in your life."

It was a seemingly heartless piece of surgery. But I felt that, like many another surgical operation, it was necessary to save life. Carroll was first of all a painter. He could dispense with food for a while, but he could not dispense with the materials of his craft. Well! The paint was out of the tubes, and it must either be utilized or wasted. So Carroll used it, with the result that his picture was not only well hung, but was sold for enough to repay the cost of the colors fifty-fold. Not long since I met him again and he assured me that his whole success as a painter dated from that lesson.

But there is another form of courage which is more important than either of those referred to – and that is moral courage – the ability to stand squarely upon your own feet and say. "Thus do I see the thing, and thus will I paint it." Look at Winslow Homer and at Whistler. Do you imagine for an instant that either of these masters ever concerned himself with the question of how anyone else saw nature? Their pictures say, hardily, "This is the way that I see it." Stick to your own vision therefore, if you would rise above the throng. Stand aloof! and force the note, if possible your own personal note. But first of all, be sure that you have something to say; for an empty boast awakes only a smile, and a bluff is soon called.

·XVI·

The Subconscious Servant

Has it ever occurred to you to inquire who it is that mechanically writes your letters for you while *you* do the thinking; who plays the notes of the piano or the violin while the musician is intent upon the interpretation; who frequently goes on reading the printed page when your thoughts have wandered far away? It is the subconscious servant, the eager helper, who performs for us daily a thousand little unrecognized services, saves our lives often by the rapidity of his action, and watches over us with constant care lest, by our own thoughtlessness, we come to any harm – the willing assistant, without whose tireless aid we could none of us support the strain of a single day's existence.

The human brain is divided into two entirely separate compartments, which might be compared to the two stories of a mansion, in the upper of which resides the lord and master who does all of the planning and ordering, while the ground floor is inhabited by the well-trained servant, who not only carries out the orders that are telephoned down from above, but, without any direct commands, attends to all the mechanical details of the household, protects the master from outside invasion, and watches over his physical needs – the conscious ego and the subconscious servant. But if the servant is to be a thoroughly capable and intelligent assistant, he must be well and carefully trained; and this fact is so well recognized that the years of our adolescence are mainly devoted to this object.

In order to appreciate how well the work is carried out and how attentively the pupil has listened to his master, you have only to call upon him for, say, the letters of the alphabet or the multiplication table. He will reel them off for you at a rate to make the head spin. He has charge of all the stored-up information of life; he is the guardian of the treasures of memory, and he keeps his treasures all pigeon-holed and tabulated, and ready for the instant service of the master – but upon one condition – that his services be so frequently called upon that his powers do not become atrophied through lack of use. It is not in the simple capacity of a bookkeeper, however, that he serves us best. Having personal charge of all our stores of knowledge and experience, he is able to correlate quickly, and can often hand us in a flash the solution of a problem which the reasoning ego might have taken hours to reach, or might never have been able to reach at all. There are numerous records of cases where mathematicians or other searchers after truth, having labored long and fruitlessly to solve a certain problem, have waked up some morning with the solution clear before them. The little subconscious servant had taken the thing up during the night and handed them the answer in the morning. The subconscious never sleeps. It is only the reasoning part of our brains that needs the recuperation of slumber.*

Genius is the term by which we designate the man or woman who is gifted with a sub-conscious nature of unusual power or activity; for the so-called flashes of genius represent the beautiful and perfect correlations and harmonies that can only be compassed at the source of things, and without the bungling interference of reasoning man. Instinct, intuition, and inspiration are other words which we use to describe this phenomenon, but they all mean the same thing.

There is no man, probably, who has more need of the help of this faithful subconscious servant than the artist, for so many of the mental processes of art must be instinctive. Moreover, in the purely mechanical sense, painters, and especially landscape painters, are peculiarly dependent upon a well trained memory. When I was a student in Paris a certain celebrated painter was helpful to me in many ways and gave me much good advice. I was in his studio one day, a month or so after his return from a trip in Holland. He placed upon the easel one after another eight finished pictures and showed me a dozen canvases rubbed in with the warm gray which he preferred for an undertone. "Those also are finished," he said; "all that remains is to put on the color." Each picture represented a different time of day, the effects varying from high noon to midnight. The motives had been stored carefully in the memory and the pictures all painted after the master's return to Paris.

It was a marvellous feat to have carried all these varying effects simultaneously in the mind without confusion, and I did not dissimulate my astonishment.

"Well, *mon ami*," he said, "I discovered when I was quite a youngster that all of the really beautiful effects, the things which I particularly wished to paint, would not wait my pleasure. They were often evanescent moods that lasted but ten minutes at most, – or they were night scenes. So I began to make studies from memory – one little study every day. After five years of this training I found that I could reproduce fairly well any scene which I had been able to study for ten minutes; and now after twenty-five years of practice my memory has become automatic; so that if I fail with any of my canvases it is not because my memory fails me but because of technical difficulties or poor judgment in the selection of the motive. On several occasions I have painted effects seen from the window of a flying train. I should advise you to begin the same kind of study."

I took his advice, and after twenty five years of the same kind of practice I can at least corroborate his statement in regard to the automatic working of the thoroughly trained memory.

But even where the effect is more lasting, and where a painter might have two or three hours to work direct from nature, I believe that the final picture must *always* be painted from memory; and I seriously question if any really great landscape was ever wholly painted in the open. A picture painted direct from nature must necessarily be hasty, ill-considered, somewhat raw, and lacking in the synthetic and personal quality which is the distinguishing

*See the very remarkable book on "Sleep," by Hon. John Bigelow.

mark of all great art – unless indeed the work is really done from memory while the painter is standing before nature – which might be the case if he had had time and opportunity to ripen his vision.

Of course one must paint what one sees, but one must see through the mind as well as through the eye. I do not mean by this to assert that young painters can entirely dispense with study direct from nature, or even that the veteran would not do well occasionally to carry his easel into the open air. The student indeed must paint for many years direct from his subject, must pry as closely as ever he can into the secrets of nature; but I would have him at the same time constantly train the sub-conscious servant, so that when the time comes that his services shall be needed, he will be indeed a "good and faithful servant."

The wonderful synthetic charm of Japanese art is largely due to the universal custom of the Japanese artists of working wholly from memory. Anyone who studies their drawings of birds, of fishes, of animals, and of flowers would find it hard to maintain (as I have heard it maintained in regard to memory painting) that they thereby lose the character of the subject. It is only when the memory is deficient or insufficient that this danger arises. A pretty story illustrative of this is told of an American traveller who, while in Tokyo, had purchased an embroidered picture of a waterfall which he desired to have appropriately framed before leaving Japan. He was directed to the workshop of an expert wood-carver, who accepted the commission; and after consultation a design was selected whose principal decorative motive was the tortoise. Returning in a couple of days, the patron found the artist at work upon the nearly completed frame, which was indeed a beautiful and most artistic creation. While they talked, something stirred among the shavings at the back of the bench. It was a live turtle which had served the carver for a model. The poor man was all blushing confusion.

"The honorable gentleman will pardon me," he said. "I am a simple artisan. Had I been an artist I should not have needed the turtle here to copy from."

One of my own most interesting and illuminating experiences was an interview which I once had with an eminent Japanese artist. At the time of my visit he was at work upon a large screen of which the principal motive was a crouching leopard ready to spring. I watched him as with three or four long supple sweeps of the brush he placed the beast upon the silken background, a marvel of sinuous and savage force.

"It is a wonder!" I exclaimed. "How do you do it?"

Oki smiled.

"In Nippon," he said, "we do not study art in the American way. We don't sit down before a thing and copy it. The master takes his pupils to the cage of the tiger, and he say: 'Look at the tiger's leg and the shape of his paws; look at his eyes and the way his ears lie back upon the head; look at his long body and his sweeping tail; see how he crouches as he walks.' Then we go home and each one makes a drawing, and the master say all those drawings very bad. And the next day we go again to the cage of the tiger and look at the things we do not remember; and we go again the next day, and maybe we go every day for one month, two month, three month – but in the end we know that tiger." And he certainly did know his tiger.

To the figure painter, of course, and especially to the painter of indoor subjects, who can control his effect and can place his model day after day in the same light, the advantage of memory painting may not be so apparent; yet even here I maintain that its more frequent use would be of greater advantage than is appreciated at the first blush; and this because the psychology of art is universal in its application, and true synthetic beauty is not within the reach of the mere copyist – be he ever so brilliant a workman.

It is said that Rembrandt often worked upon his pictures from memory, and report has it that Velasquez preferred to paint with his sitter in the next room. In regard to the greatest of all modem figure painters, and one of the greatest of all times, Jean François Millet, we have living witnesses to the fact that he never worked from nature.

Now if this is held to be bad and dangerous counsel to give to students, I would simply remark that a student is a potential master, that he has the right to all the knowledge there is in the world, and that he must be presumed to have sufficient discretion to apply it wisely to his own needs. Coddling never developed a strong man.

For more information about training one's visual memory, see *Memory Drawing: Perceptual Training and Recall*, by Darren R. Rousar.

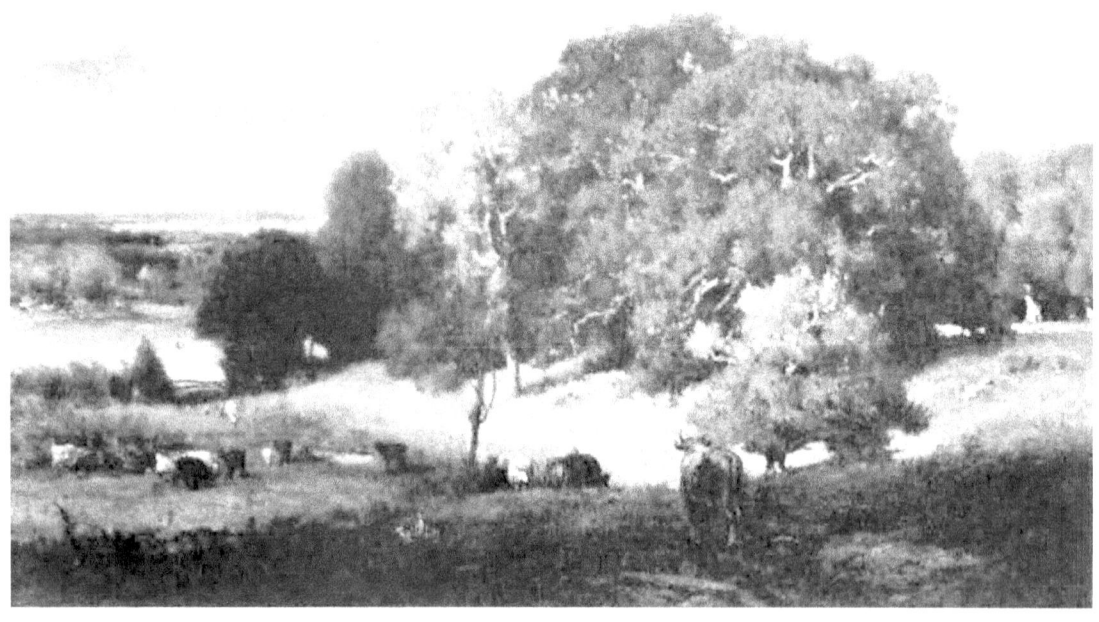

George Inness
Autumn Oaks

·XVII·

Temperament

Atalented young painter, who was just beginning to make his mark, drifted into my studio one day and threw himself into a chair in gloomy silence. He smoked morosely for five minutes, while I went on with my painting. Finally he broke the silence. "Have I told you," he said, "that I mean to give up art, to quit the whole bally business? Well! it is a fact. I have had the offer of an excellent berth in my father's office, and I am going to accept it."

"Why! why!" I cried, "what is all this coil?"

"That is precisely what I am unable to explain," he replied. "I have simply lost my grip. I have forgotten how to paint, and that is all there is to it. I am in first-class shape physically and my brain-box doesn't show any unusual cracks; but for the past two months my work has been going from bad to worse. Every canvas is just a little more like punk than the preceding one. At first I gritted my teeth and worked all the harder; but the harder I worked the worse my things became. It's no use. I throw up the sponge."

I dropped my palette and grasped him by the hand with an enthusiasm which must have appeared to him somewhat misplaced. "My dear fellow," I cried, "I congratulate you. If your pictures had not already shown you the consummate painter, you have just given the most incontrovertible proof of the fact. You are simply soaked in temperament. Get down on your knees, my boy, and thank your lucky stars for that. If the pendulum has swung unconscionably low at present, you may rest assured that it will swing all the higher on the return stroke. The only man who never doubts himself, who plugs stolidly on to his goal, deviating neither to right nor to left, is the man who is born wholly without temperament. If he never falls to any depths of despair, neither does he rise to any heights of glory; and if he is never supremely miserable, on the other hand he is never supremely happy. He is simply the good, honest bromide; the very salt of the earth, if you will, and its balance-wheel; but never by any conceivable possibility could he be an artist. Your present depression is simply the price that you pay for the immense joy which is yours during the full tide of creative production. So take your medicine like a man. Also take a drink if you need it, but let us hear no more of this drivel about giving up art."

As artists grow older, and after a dozen repetitions of the same experience, they come to regard this recurrent waxing and waning of the divine flame as a normal condition of their being; and presently they recognize the fits of depression as periods of incubation, out of which they are apt to emerge with added strength, with some new light on difficult problems that have long harassed them. They also discover that these off times can be very profitably employed in many ways – in absorbing the great literature of the world for instance, a pleasure for which they have scant leisure at other times; in studying the great masters of painting and delving after the secret of their greatness; and last, but not least, in simple physical relaxation and recuperation – tramps across the hills or bouts on the golf-links – the eye always open and the mind passively but delightfully receptive.

One of our very greatest painters, who is now gone, never learned this important lesson. When the flame burned low, and work lagged, he drank coffee to stimulate his tired nerves. When even this failed to rouse the exhausted energies he had recourse to alcohol, and when finally the great work was completed the painter was often launched upon a spree of a fortnight's duration. It thus happens that a man who temperamentally disliked alcohol, who was normally one of the gentlest and soberest of men, has gone down in history as a roysterer and a dipsomaniac. He burned himself out before his time; but in thus recklessly using up his vital energies, he produced a series of wonderful pictures that will remain for all time one of the chief glories of our day. In the final summing up, when reputations are resorted and re-classed, he will be given his true place; and it will be the place of a great if a mistaken hero.

But most of us have now grown wiser. In either literature or art it is no longer considered necessary unduly to burn the midnight oil or to wear the hair long. And when the inevitable fits of temperamental depression are upon us we have learned that the only thing to do is to keep a level head, to see things in their true proportions, and to trust in the Lord – to be a philosopher, in a word. I do not mean a philosopher of the cold and aristocratic Nietzsche type, nor a pessimist like Schopenhauer, but a genial, sane, and whole-souled optimist like Socrates. All true philosophers are levellers – levellers up as well as down. A condition of affairs which might loom portentous and threatening to the man in the street, such as one would receive with a smile of gentle humor, for he would see through the disguise and know it as a harmless humbug; while something else which to the ordinary mortal might appear a mere triviality he would lift gravely into a place of high honor, divining its fundamental seriousness and importance.

These regularly recurring fits of depression seem to depend in no wise upon the state of the bodily health. In Robert Louis Stevenson and Theodore Robinson we have examples of wonderful temperamental resilience coupled with wretched physical condition.

In fact, as a noted painter once said to me, "These semi-invalids neither need nor deserve our commiseration, for in reality the beggars have the advantage of us. *Their* nerves are always sensitive and keyed to pitch, while we husky chaps have to flog ours up to the point. We must dig painfully through the outer layers of flesh and muscle before we can get at the spirit, while the invalids are all spirit. Personally, I know that my best work is always done the morning after a spree, when I come to the studio a bit shaky and with the nerves all on edge."

Although this highly immoral statement was evidently made largely with a view to picturesque effect, it did, nevertheless, enunciate a truth that has generally escaped attention; for it is quite true that (given sufficient strength to drag the body about) physical weakness is not an insuperable bar to success in art. Very frail men and very frail women have achieved distinction in various artistic callings. This, however, applies more particularly to the sedentary arts, such as writing, musical composition, and certain lines of crafts work: for the painter, and especially the landscape painter must sometimes cover miles with his legs in the course of his day's work. We all know also that a robust physique is essential to success on the operatic stage.

Nor do the spells of depression of which we are speaking appear to derive in any way from the dominating and conscious portion of our brains – the part which under great physical or emotional strain sometimes loses its balance; for there are cases of artists who have become insane and have still remained great artists. A noted example of this kind was the Spaniard Goya. The character of his subjects was affected by his loss of mental control, naturally. They became ghastly and often incoherent. This was what might have been expected. But the fundamental temperamental quality of his art remained great, to the end. The temperamental man, dwelling deep down below the surface, had not been affected by the storm which had played havoc with the surface nature.

We are therefore forced irresistibly to the conclusion that temperament resides in the emotional, in other words, in the subconscious nature of man. When the temperamental energy gives out, and the artist loses his grip, the strong probability is that he has, without knowing it, overworked the subconscious servant; and if this ever faithful helper fails to respond to the demands made upon him, it is through no unwillingness to serve the master, but because of utter exhaustion and inability to react.

If therefore we regard these periods of temperamental depression as incomprehensible, it is because we have come to look upon the conscious, reasoning part of our intelligence as the sole source of mental energy, whereas it is only one factor in the complicated organism which we know as the human ego. If we cared to push still further our researches along this same line, we might claim that above and beyond both the conscious and the subconscious natures of man lives the animating and controlling essence from which both must draw their power, and which, for lack of a better nomenclature, we call the human soul. But this is the job of the psychologist, not of the artist.

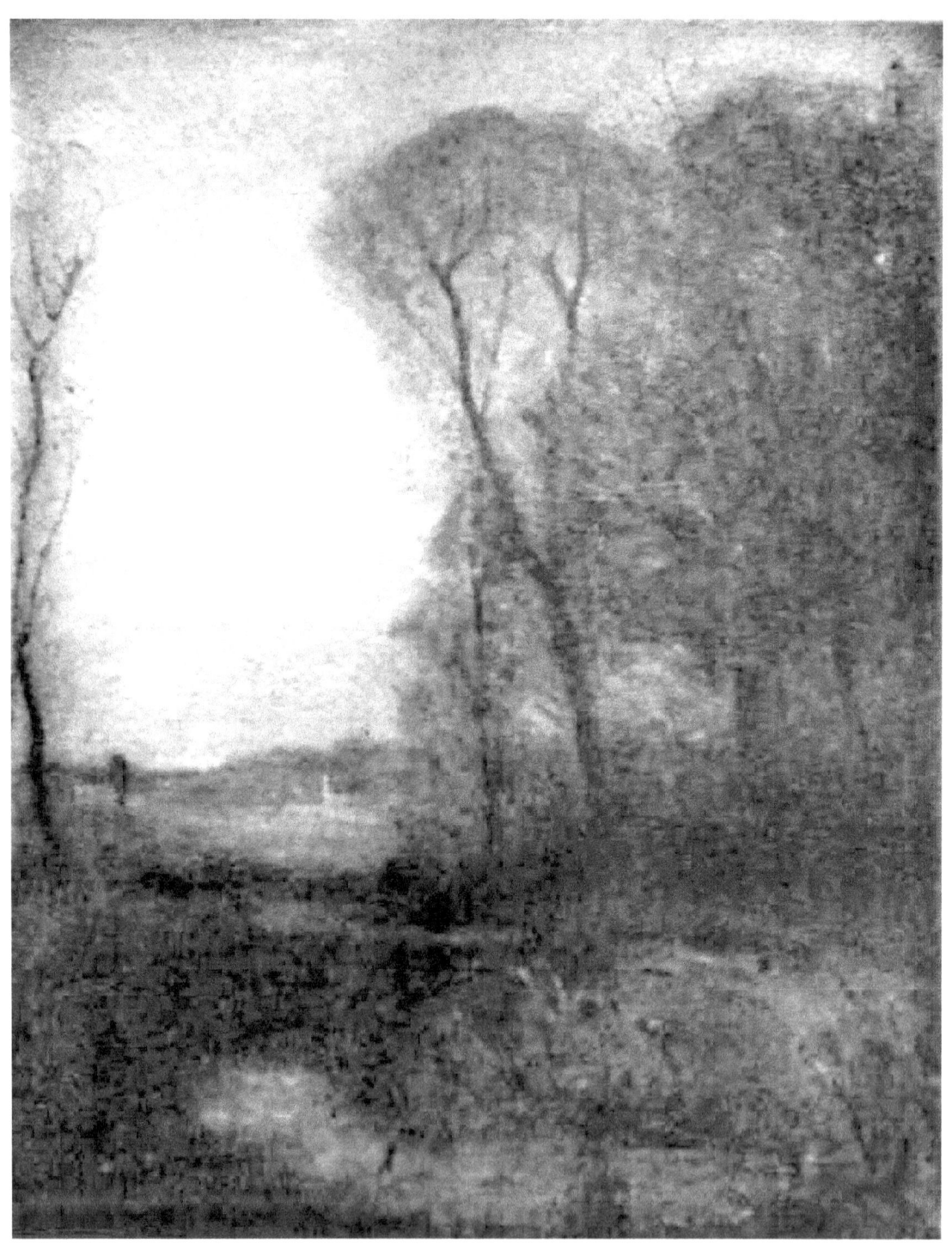

Charles Melville Dewey
October Evening

·XVIII·

Character

If you should ask a dozen painters what mental qualification was most essential to an artist's success, the chances are that every man of them would reply "temperament" – in other words, genius and imagination. Transposed, these terms all mean the same thing – a peculiarly sensitive subconscious organization – one that is at once keenly alive to beauty, and capable of that rapid and intuitive coordination of impressions whose visible and tangible result is the work of genius. And in a way the painters would be right; for without temperament no man can be an artist; but temperament alone will not suffice. If I were myself asked to supply a formula for the making of an artist, my receipt would be, one part genius and nine parts hard work. I sometimes glance back to my student days and wonder what has become of all the clever and brilliant chaps over whose easels the rest of us were used to hang in awe and admiration. One by one they have all dropped out. Things came too easy to them. They were not *obliged* to "plug" and "grind," and so they never learned their trade. Their places have been taken by others – the plodders who stuck to their studies throughout the whole week with grim determination, dropping their brushes only at the stroke of twelve on Saturday. One ugly duckling in particular I remember well. His work was so hopeless that the whole Latin Quarter was sincerely sorry for him. Finally his master in despair urged him to give up art and go into the grocery line. That man is at present one of the most famous artists of the day – a truly great painter. Down deep in his nature, of course, he had temperament. He could not have achieved his distinguished place in art without it. But he also had *character*; character, which means the ability to work when it would be easier to play; the ability to say "No," when it would be far easier to say "Yes"; the ability to stand out in the sun and sweat over a study when it would be so much pleasanter to lie in the shade and read a book; the ability to live on a dollar a week and be content; the ability to surrender all of the little present pleasures of life, in order one day to achieve that greater pleasure which comes with success in one's chosen profession.

I met recently a schoolboy companion who as a man has won an enviable position in life. He told me that at one time he was a cub engineer in the employ of Andrew Carnegie. An important part of one of the important machines having broken, he was detailed to secure a duplicate fitting, with stringent orders to return with the missing part before nightfall. He hustled off with the determination to make a record, and scoured both Pittsburg and Allegheny City without result. He then telephoned to Cincinnati, Cleveland and Louisville with no better success. Finally he called up New York; and there at last got on the track of the much wanted cam. He could have caught a late afternoon train and been back in the morning, but, all things considered, he thought it would be best to report at headquarters, and then take the midnight express if ordered to do so. He was pretty proud of himself on the whole, and did not mind having missed his dinner. Seeking out Mr. Carnegie he started in to tell him all that he had done in his strenuous day. The iron master interrupted him brusquely.

"Young man," he said, "I care nothing for explanations. I demand results. I will give you another twenty four hours. If by that time you have not procured the cam, you leave the works."

My friend left the iron master's presence somewhat crestfallen; but he then and there made up his mind to demand as much of himself in future as was now demanded of him. He never failed again in a serious undertaking; and he rose to be one of the chief steel experts of the country, with an income anywhere from $50,000 to $100,000 a year.

Now if that kind of character and determination are necessary to success in business life, they are infinitely more necessary to an artist. He has no taskmaster to hold him to his job. He is the slave of no factory bell or whistle. No desk or office calls him daily at 9 A.M. He is as free as the air to come and go as he likes, and when he likes. He can work as little or as much as he pleases. He can loaf at his own sweet will. And for this very reason, he is in honor bound to work, and to work hard and seriously. It is a case of *noblesse oblige*.

Moreover, it is a case of necessity. If you would "arrive," you must work always to the limit of your force – and just a little beyond. It is not all cakes and ale. There is no especial fun for instance in grinding away month after month, and year after year, at drawing, which is not your forte; in cramming up on values, refraction and other technical things which are not always remarkably interesting, but which you *must* have at your finger-ends before you can "let yourself go." And even when you have reached that happy stage, the necessity for hard and unremitting labor has not ceased. Sargent will tell you that he has frequently scraped out a single head twenty times. For the optimistic student who looks forward to the happy time when the necessity for hard work shall be ended there is inscribed over the portals of the palace of art this special motto: "All hope abandon ye who enter here."

A young painter once stood behind the veteran Jules Breton, while he was at work upon one of his important pictures – his favorite subject of little maids in their white communion robes. It was delightful to observe the ease and dexterity of his every stroke. The youth spoke enviously of the joy it must be to have attained to his perfect facility of technic and to know every time a picture was begun that it could be carried through easily to a successful end.

"My dear boy," was the reply, "you will never reach that happy land here below. I sweat blood over every one of my pictures, and there is never a one that is not at some time a failure. Every new picture brings a new problem, and who knows if we may be able to solve it. But if there were no new problems we should all cease painting; for there would be no more art."

The true artist, after all, is greedy for work. He needs no spur to goad him to his best endeavor. The danger lies upon the other side. Cazin used to say, "An artist has no time to care for his health." And this is literally true; for the conditions of artistic creation often demand that a painter or a sculptor shall frequently work far beyond the limits of his strength during a long period – shall draw heavy drafts upon the future; and these drafts must either be paid by a shortened life, or made up later by prolonged periods of rest. As it is not possible for the artist to work as other men work, a given number of hours each day, this hardest of all workers frequently gains the reputation of being an idler.

I cannot think, however, that erratic hours are either necessary or excusable in the routine of *student* life. The student's business is to learn all he can – to train the subconscious servant to be the valuable helper that he must needs be later on; and this can be done day by day with as much adherence to regular hours as the businessman demands of his assistants. Moreover, the habit thus acquired will tend to reduce to a minimum the irregularity which to a certain extent is inevitable later on. Let the student who feels within his soul the divine fire of genius beware of pitfalls. If he is wise, he will bottle up that fire for future use, and in the meantime apply himself (like the diligent apprentice) to the acquisition of knowledge.

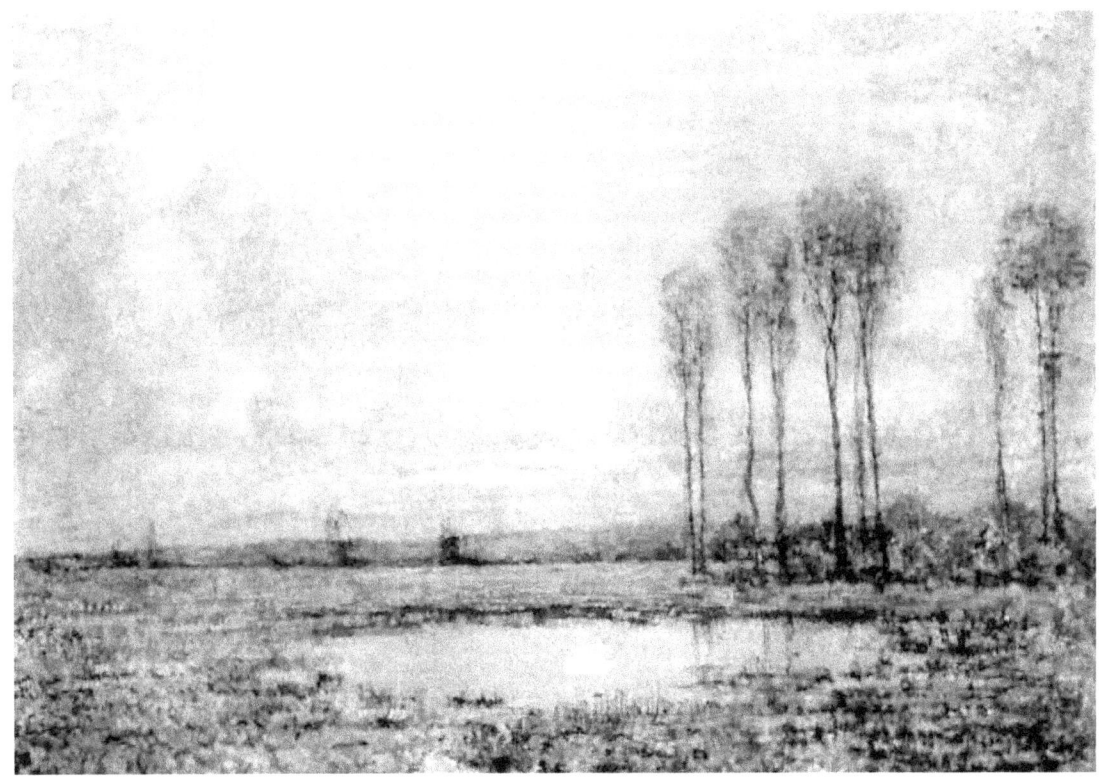

Henry G. Dearth
Moonrise

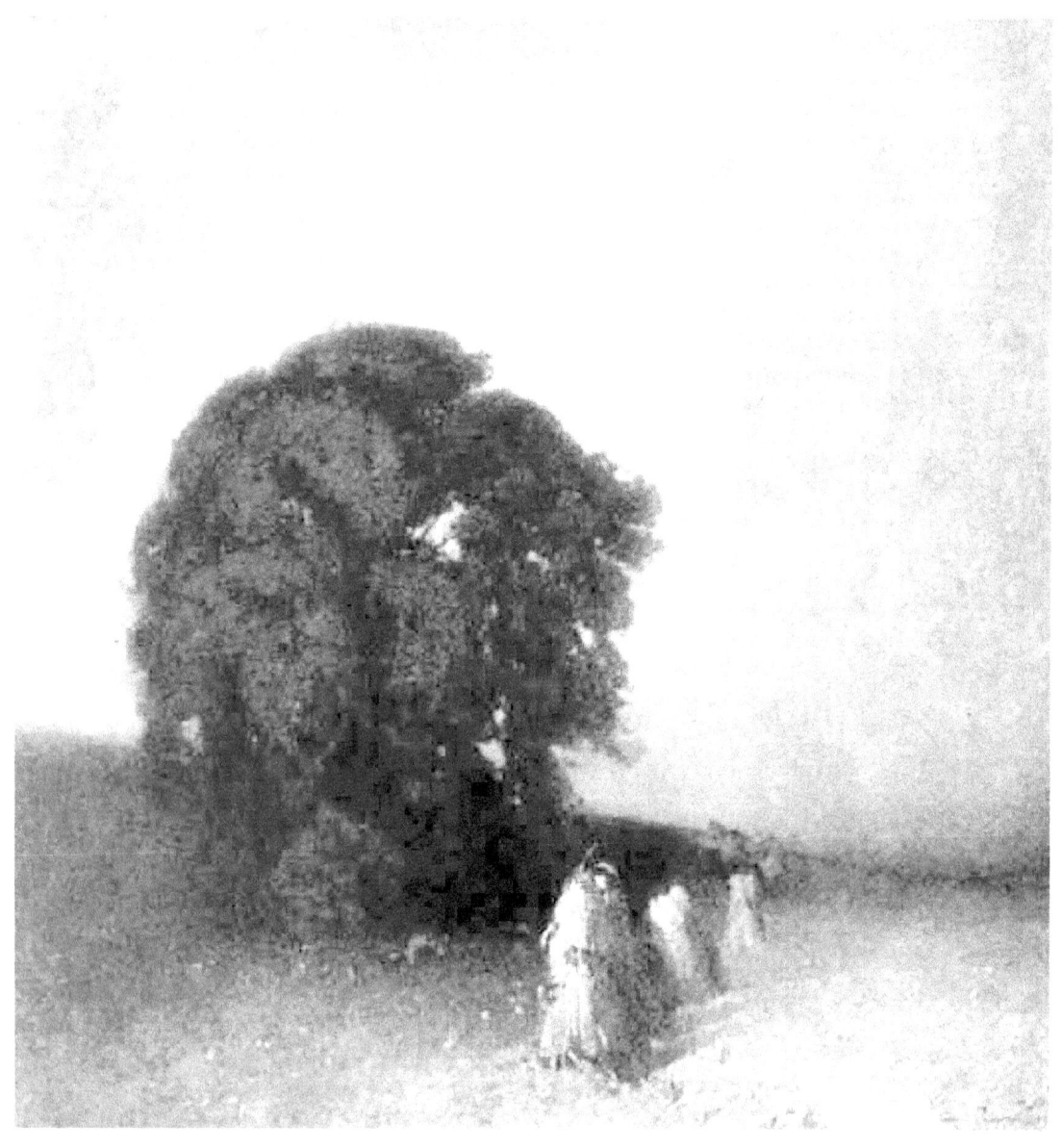

Emil Carlsen
Landscape

·XIX·

What is a Good Picture?

In reply to the above question almost any painter would reply "mine own"; and if the particular painter to whom the question is put chances to be gifted with sufficient temperament, backed by a sufficient training, his claim might very well be justified. But there is an equal chance that his judgment would be at fault in the matter, for artists are notoriously the poorest judges of their own work. All painters willingly concede the correctness of this statement as applied to their brother artists, but there are few, indeed, who will admit its justice when applied to themselves. If this were otherwise the rule which has for years made the exhibitions of the National Academy of Design the poorest of their kind in the United States – that provision which exempts from the action of the jury certain pictures entered by Academicians and Associates – would long since have been abrogated; for, just as no man willingly or wittingly writes himself down an ass, so no painter would wittingly brand himself a duffer. In spite of this peculiar personal blindness (which seems to be incidental to the artistic temperament) when it comes to the work of other artists, painters are the best judges of painting. Of course due allowance must be made for personal idiosyncrasy and variation of taste. In art, as in music or gastronomy, taste varies infinitely according to individual temperament, or training. But just as a wise gourmet, to whose palate terrapin makes no special appeal, would not, for that only reason, deny it a place upon the bill of fare, so no sensible painter would deny the artistic value of a Japanese print or a Persian rug simply because he does not happen to make that brand of art. Indeed, if there is any one rule for the judgment of works of art whose application is universal, it is that which demands of a picture, a print or a ceramic that it shall differ from all other work in the same line, that it shall bear the impress not only of race but of individual personality within the racial limits. For it is the personality which makes the art. Nature, however beautiful, is not art. Art is natural beauty interpreted through human temperament.

Here, then, we have at least one infallible test, which can be applied to any work under discussion – that it shall be clearly and strongly stamped with the personality of its maker, so that we may know without asking that a drawing is by Hokusai, or a painting by Velasquez, Whistler, or Winslow Homer. And originality thus expressed is only another word for sincerity. Sincerity used in this sense, however, is far from meaning a slavish or mechanical copy of nature. The highest form of sincerity is truth to the artist's own personal vision of beauty.

All true art is the direct result of analysis and synthesis on the part of the artist – whether instinctive, or accomplished with a clear conception of the work to be done. Having analyzed nature's suggestive motive, the artist is at liberty in the synthetic building up of his work to use as many or as few of the elements as his personal sense of beauty tells him will be necessary to the work in hand. He can employ the whole scale or he can reduce his choice to the few conventional symbols used in a beautiful Persian rug; the only imperative law being that he shall go direct to nature for his inspiration; the inevitable penalty of failure in this respect being the limbo of the imitator – the loss of all freshness, spontaneity, and personality. With this one restriction the artist's latitude is practically unlimited, for in a general sense art is any object made by man which is conceded by his fellow-man to be beautiful.

In regard to the picture, it is difficult to foresee at present just how far the average cultivated person will follow the artist into the region of pure symbolism; how few of the elements he will demand, and how much his own imagination will supply. When we remember that less than a generation ago the work of Corot and of Millet was nearly incomprehensible to the cultivated French public; that even the artist juries refused it admission to the Salon; that twenty years since those who freely accepted the work of Monet and Sisley were few indeed, we may confidently look forward to a time when only the most essential symbols of beauty will be required of the artist. But what exact direction this synthetic development will take we can only conjecture at the present time. Whether Matisse and his followers in France today are the true prophets crying in the wilderness the future alone can demonstrate. If this group finally makes good it will be because they have discovered something which is fundamentally true and human, something which is sincerely (if blindly) desired by the race at large. It is quite certain that no abnormality masquerading under the name of the "art of the future" will win a permanent place in the regards of humanity. The beauty which is to endure must be sane and wholesome, because the human race is sound at heart and can be counted upon in the long run to reject anything which is essentially unhealthy or decadent.

In the meantime all our aesthetic experience points to the fact that the new beauty does not destroy our love or appreciation of the old. A picture by Rembrandt or Velasquez meets today with as much admiration as if the "luminarist" or the "symbolist" school had not arisen. A thing that is once truly beautiful is always beautiful; and the painters of today can remain calmly confident that if they are true to their own ideals and to the spirit of their times, their output will be accorded the same meed of praise by future generations that we today give to the work of the old masters.

·XX·

The True Impressionism

When instantaneous photography was first discovered, some thirty years ago, high hopes of it were entertained by the artists. It was thought, for instance, that it would prove of inestimable value to such painters as Meissonier and Schreyer, men who delighted to portray the horse in violent action. But to the surprise of everybody these great expectations were not fulfilled. At first, the artists themselves were puzzled to account for this and to explain why the curiously contorted attitudes now disclosed for the first time, conveyed so little the impression of motion. But when the instantaneous photographs were subjected to a process of selection and elimination, it was finally discovered that there were practically but two instants in the stride of the galloping horse that conveyed any idea of rapid flight to the human eye. The first of these was at the very beginning of the stride, when, with all four legs bunched together under the belly, the animal was preparing for the forward leap; and the second was at the end of the impulse, when, with legs outstretched to the limit, the horse was ready to take the ground again for another stride. Both of these periods, it will be seen, were the instants of arrest at motion – instants when the human eye could readily seize the action without the intervention of the kodak. Then at last was perceived the fundamental law which underlay the phenomenon: the human eye, and the human brain behind it, declined to accept as a symbol of motion anything which the eye had not been able to see for and by itself unaided. In this case, of course, it was only during the two instants of arrest of motion that the eye had been able to note the position of the horse's limbs. And these two positions of comparative inaction had, through long association, become the permanent and fixed symbols of action in the racing horse. The kodak had revealed hitherto unsuspected facts and aspects of motion, but the eye would have none of them, and clung only to that which was visual.

It was this experience with the earliest kodaks which finally made plain the reason why, from time out of mind, artists desiring to convey the concept of motion had instinctively chosen the end or the beginning of the stroke or impulse – the axe poised in mid-air ready for its downward sweep, or the stroke completed in the heart of the tree – the lifting wave poised for the fall, or the breaker that has crashed to its turbulent end upon the beach. Shortly also, it began to be seen that the marine painter who depended upon the kodak for his drawing, lost all sense of motion in the waves, that the wind-blown drapery of a photograph was nearly as rigid as a sheet of crumpled tin; that the impression, in fact, which the eye received from nature was not that which was rendered by the camera; and that, therefore, the human brain could never accept the photograph as a thoroughly satisfactory transcript of nature.

It is to be feared that the hopes which are at present being built upon color photography are doomed to like disappointment – for the simple reason that the photographic lens in no way resembles the lens of the human eye. The very fact that it is a more perfect instrument is against it. It gives us scientific facts; and scientific facts are generally artistic lies. Art has nothing to do with things as they are, but only with things as they *appear* to be, with the visual not the actual, with *impressions*, not with realities. It is a scientific fact, for instance, that trees are green, and yet it is only under the rarest combination of favoring circumstances that a tree is really green to the visual sense. It is much more likely to be pearly-gray or royal-purple or rich amber or sapphire blue, according as it happens to be seen under the pale effulgence of dawn, the shimmering blaze of noonday, the golden glow of sunset or the azure mystery of night. And it is the same with every other landscape feature under the great blue arch of heaven. Each rock, each tree, each waving field of grain has, of course, its fixed and definite local color, but the *appearance* of each of these objects changes a thousand times a day. And it is with this equation – this fleeting, intangible, ever-shifting, ever-varying *appearance*, that artists have to do. The *facts* of nature are to him nothing, the mood everything.

By an ironical chance he has it in his power to convince the most uncompromising and unimaginative scientific purist of the truth of his statement that the most unquestionable facts of science are often the most shameless of visual lies – and this by the simplest sort of a *scientific* demonstration. In the diagram [on the following page], two upright lines of equal length are traced side by side, and near enough together to allow of easy visual comparison. To No.1 have been affixed at top and bottom a pair of divergent wings extending upward and downward away from the centre. To No. 2 the same wings have been affixed, but their direction has been reversed so that they extend toward the centre of the diagram instead of away from it. Now no amount of didactic statement will convince the human eye that those two central lines are of the same length. Here the scientific fact has become a visual lie. If an artist should by any chance be using these two forms as units in a decorative frieze wherein it was essential that they should be of the same length, he would unhesitatingly lengthen the central line of No. 2 and shorten that of No. I, so that visually they would become equal; and in so doing he would be telling the truth in his own way; whereas had he allowed the foot-rule to control him he would have been guilty of an artistic lie.

The Greek architects, observing that the horizontal architrave surmounting the columns on their temples *appeared* to sag, corrected the fault by giving their architrave a slightly upward arch, thus by means of a curve securing a straight line; or at least a line which was architecturally and visually straight.

Here then clearly lies the division line between science and art – the one gives us actual truths, the other visual truths; the one facts, the other moods, impressions, visions;

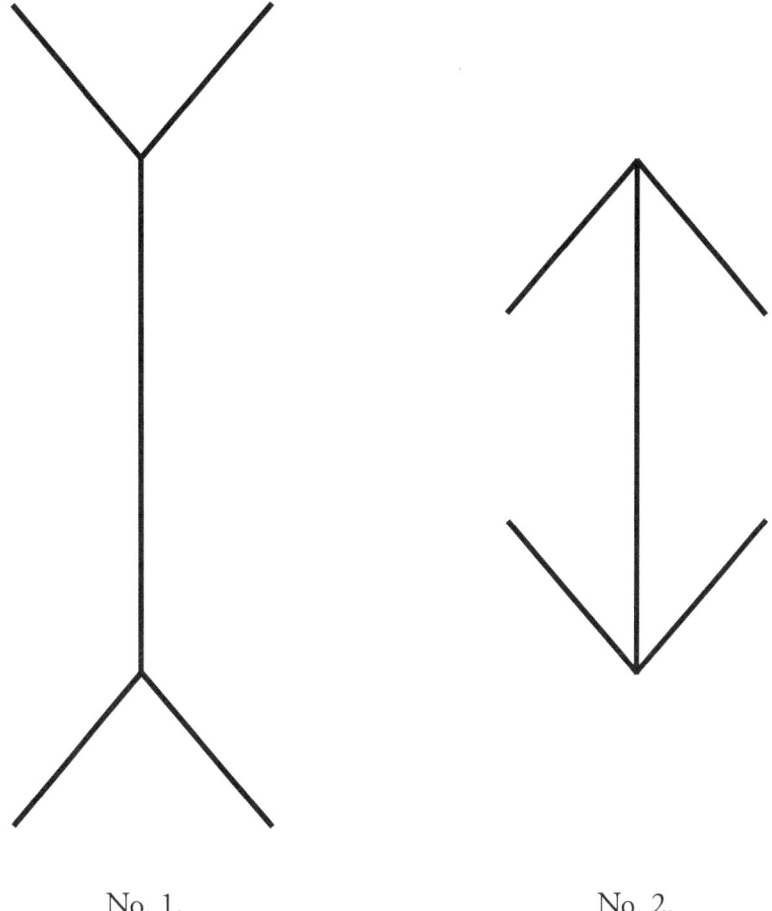

No. 1.   No. 2.

each in its place admirable, each ministering to one of the two great needs of humanity, the physical and the spiritual. If only a pact could be signed between them, by the terms of which each should agree to abide peaceably within the bounds of its own legitimate sphere, all would be well. But alas! science is a conscienceless freebooter. So much the sturdier of the two, he encroaches constantly on the domain of art; insists on recognition where he has no right to a hearing, and monopolizes the whole front of the stage. Even the artists are unable to escape his importunities; and the younger ones especially are often misled and lured to a false allegiance.

This is small wonder of course, when you remember that ever since the day of our birth we have been storing our minds with thousands upon thousands of facts – very useful facts, too, in their way, facts whose possession and unconscious daily use are essential to our very physical existence. But when, as artists, we go into the open, to study and to dream, they rise before us like a miasma, a deadly cloud that obscures the whole face of nature; so that we see the landscape not as it is, but as we have been taught in some former stage of existence that it should be.

Among the facts that have thus been clamped upon us there are two alas! which have been learned by everybody – that trees are green and that the sky is blue. It matters not that the sky is often pale green, or violet, or pearl-gray or opal, *blue* it is painted forever and forever; and the trees are painted green. And these blue and green monstrosities not only find a ready sale but much loving appreciation. There are in the world so many others who as children learned that the sky was blue and the trees were green and have never since opened their eyes. To tell the truth, so strong is the hold upon us of these early traditions that it takes many years of the severest training to overcome them. In many cases, and not infrequently in the case of some truly great painter, the fifty-year mark is chalked up against him before the scales fall utterly from his eyes and he is able at length to look out straight before him with a vision that is clear and un-obscured. Take my word for it, technique is not the difficult thing in art. Any reasonably capable youth can readily master all of the technical problems in existence in a few short months, but it requires many a long and weary year to learn to *see*.

And to think that but for those stored-up facts it would all have been so easy. If painters, gazing upon nature, could only look forth with the simplicity of a new-born child, which opens its eyes for the first time on a fresh and virgin world, the principal problem of art would be solved in an instant. Give us, Oh, Lord! to see! and we will find the means of expression.

It is a simple platitude to say that an artist can always paint as much as he sees. All of the fumbling, and struggle, and hard work connected with a picture comes of the effort to see just a little more, just a little better. Technique truly is mere child's play. It is a question, moreover, if too much technique is not a serious handicap to any artist – if indeed it does not tend to degrade him to the level of the mere handcraftsman. At any rate, Millet's previously quoted saying to the effect that technique should never open shop for itself, that it should always hide modestly behind the idea to be expressed is one of the eternal truths of art. In the work of his own great period the technique is so rough as to prove conclusively his – personal contempt for mere surface quality. And this crudity must have been voluntary. We may go even further and say that it was *intentional*; for in his own brilliant youth there were none so clever, none so *habile* as he.

In the case of our own Winslow Homer also, the thing to be said is often so vital, the vision so clear-cut, that although the paint is simply flung at the canvas, we don't care a fig. The mood has been rendered – the message has carried, and we do not stop to consider the phraseology.

But, as I have before intimated, each painter must look at all times out of his own eyes, and not through the eyes of his brother. In fact, in the modern scheme of things, the artist is the last rank individualist to survive. For him the merger and the combination spell ruin. Again we insist, and insist yet once again, that the very essence and marrow of art is personality. Any surrender of personality, therefore, can lead only to one goal – the abyss of artistic worthlessness.

Under these circumstances it becomes interesting to inquire just how much the young painter may accept with safety from his master; in what manner he may best acquire the thorough and intimate knowledge of technique which is so essential to his success, without sacrifice of that personal integrity which is still more essential. Let us at once concede the fact that there is no perfect system of art instruction. But without question the system most nearly approaching the ideal is that which has the great art school or institute for its central idea. To begin with, students learn much more from each other than they do from their masters. The constant attrition and stimulation, the wholesome emulation of the school keeps every mental fibre on the full jump, every nerve alive and tingling. The progress made by each helps the other forward. The student sees here a technical point, there a trick or an idea, and, like the young barbarian that he is, he promptly appropriates them all to his own use. And this is just so much to the good, for the callow cub is putting on technique much as a young animal puts on flesh. The system has only one serious drawback. The tendency of all schools is to develop *a school*. This is bad, because the whole intent of art training should be to develop individual artists, each differing from the other to the full breadth and extent of personal temperament. This danger, it is true, arises only toward the end of the school period when the youths' eyes are at last open and they are beginning to "take notice" of things about them. But it is nevertheless a very genuine and menacing danger, which is to be guarded against and combated in every way possible.

When in the course of human events it came my own turn to fulfil the universal duty of the older to the younger generation, I had this danger writ large before me. One day there came the inevitable little deputation of students, asking if the master would kindly consent to paint a study before the class, "just to show the way he would go about it" to obtain this effect or that. My reply, I remember, was somewhat brusque. "Not on your life," I said. "I will tell you all that I know of the fundamental principles which underlie all good art, and which are everywhere and eternally the same. I will tell you also as much as I personally know of the infinite variety of technical methods which abound in oil painting, and from which it is yours to select at will such as may best suit the temperament or the personal point of view of each of your number. But I will never do you the unkind service of putting you in the way to imitate a technique which, though serviceable to me personally, could no more fit your aesthetic needs than would an old coat of mine fit your bodies. Remember that art is nature *as the artist sees it*, and it is no more possible for two human beings to see nature in the same way than for the same two people to have exactly similar features. As our brains vary, so does our point of view. Cling desperately to your own vision, therefore. Accept no advice, take no criticism that does not harmonize with it. In this way only can you hope to be original. Turn the mind to nature like a mirror and let it reflect exactly what is thrown upon it. He who attempts to improve upon nature either lacks judgment or is endowed with a conceit so colossal that there is no health in him. Be reverent before nature and honest with yourself, and your art will ring true every time. All of you, it is true, will not sing the song of the nightingale, because you were not all born nightingales; but the blackbird's lay is sweet, and the thrush and the oriole fill the woods with melody. Even the homely robin and the linnet have modest little notes of their own which are pleasant to the ear of a dewy April morning. Of all the songsters in creation there is only one, I believe, whose lay is universally condemned – and that is the parrot."

The greater the artist, I think, the more certain is he to cling religiously to nature, not only for his *inspiration*, but for the actual material of his creations. Rodin not long since said to an interviewer, "All my attention as an artist is devoted to reproducing exactly what I see in nature. I do not endeavor to 'express something.' Those who have a pre-conceived idea – an inspiration as they call it – are seldom able to render their ideal. Those, on the contrary, who charm us by their talent have done nothing throughout the ages but reproduce nature. They copy as closely as ever they can the most beautiful, the most admirable, the most perfect thing in the world – which is nature."

This does not mean, however, that an artist must necessarily be a mere machine, that he has no intellectual liberty of choice in regard to what he shall represent and how he shall represent it. Art includes every object of intrinsic beauty that was ever created by human hands. The Turkish rug, the Chinese ceramic, the Moorish carving, the Japanese color-print and the Gothic cathedral are just as truly art in the highest sense as the Greek marble or the modern painting. But there are certain limits beyond which an artist may not step, and all art which has attained to greatness has been the sincere expression, not only of the individual artist, but of the race to which he belongs, and the epoch in which he lives. It will not do for Americans to make Oriental rugs or Japanese color-prints; and we have all seen and deplored the Japanese attempt to assimilate and reproduce our own occidental art – have shuddered indeed at the brilliant and hollow shell without a soul. Is it not enough for us to admire without attempting to imitate, to surround ourselves with the beauty of all ages and all peoples while calmly pursuing the type of beauty which it is given to us to see as none others have been able to see it? Now, if I am not much mistaken, the form of beauty which appeals to us as it has appealed to no other race in any other epoch of the world's history is the poetry of out-of-door nature, her mystery, and her ever-varying and shifting moods. Surely in this wide field there remains to us a sufficient latitude of choice both as regards the subjects we shall paint and the manner in which we shall render our impressions. It is always open to us to choose our direction. In each of us there is a Dr. Jekyll and a Mr. Hyde, and in art as in life it depends on ourselves which shall rule.

When I was a student in Paris away back in the seventies, a group of young artists who were at that time making some stir in the art world asserted with a great deal of unnecessary noise and bluster that good painting could glorify the most revolting subject. The subject was nothing, the craftsmanship everything. I remember that I was temporarily caught up in the swirl of the movement and that for a time I ran with the shouting iconoclasts; and the memory of this makes me still lenient with any youngster who raises the old cry – false as it is. It is a phase – one of the growing pains of adolescence which are normal and to be expected. If we only remember that, we shall have no cause to worry. I believe that every young painter must at some time worship at the shrine of technique, just as every youth who is to grow up to true and generous manhood must at some period of his boyish career be a socialist. But it is a sign of mental atrophy – of arrested development, when the youth or the artist fails to graduate out of this chrysalis stage.

Nature is not all beautiful by any means. But why should we choose to perpetuate her ugly side? I believe it to be one of the artist's chief functions, as it should be his chief delight, to watch for the rare mood when she wafts aside the veil of the commonplace and shows us her inner soul in some bewildering vision of poetic beauty. I should not care personally to hold a brief for the opponents of this view – nor should I know how to support it. Yet a painter of world-wide reputation once said to me that he positively hated a picture in which there was a moon. He declared that any picture which depended for its appeal upon the beauty of the subject was weak-kneed art, publicly advertising its own weakness. The very perfection of craftsmanship could not save such a picture, he said. The best and only answer to this sincere critique is that the painter who made it has remained all his life a craftsman – a craftsman of the highest distinction if you will, but never an artist.

Now from all that has been said above, it would appear that originality must be the easiest of all qualities to attain. But this is, unfortunately, not the case. The facility is only apparent. The hard and sober reality is that the personal note is the most difficult of all things for an artist to grasp and to hold. It is only necessary to count over the number of our truly original artists (it can be done upon the ten fingers) to see how true this statement is. One of the oldest of our proverbs says that to err is human. It is also human, unfortunately, to be a sheep – to do as you see others do – to imitate the thing, which you admire; and the sad result of this is that few ever learn to see the thing which lies out in the sunlight under their own very eyes. And this is why originality – why true impressionism will ever remain one of the rarest and most precious qualities in art.

Now it has doubtless been objected that the present chapter, while professing to deal with impressionism, says mighty little about the impressionists. But I have failed singularly in my intention if, by this time, I have not made it clear that anyone who honestly and sincerely records his impressions of nature *is* in the truest sense an impressionist – that Velasquez and Titian and Rembrandt were as truly impressionists as were Manet or Monet or Sisley – because, in the canvases of these great masters of the Renaissance, there rings the true note of personality – proof positive of their honesty, their reverence, and their humility before nature. To tell the truth, the so-called French impressionists were far more accurately termed luminarists, or painters of light. Their special achievement in art was a purely technical triumph – the discovery that by the use of broken color in its prismatic simplicity the pulsating, vibrating effect of light could be transferred to the surface of a canvas. But they were neither the fathers of impressionism nor were they especially distinguished in this line. As a matter of fact, they were somewhat deficient in the quality of personal vision, and their rage to secure the effect of light at all hazards led to a certain monotony of technique which tended to blunt the personal note in their work.

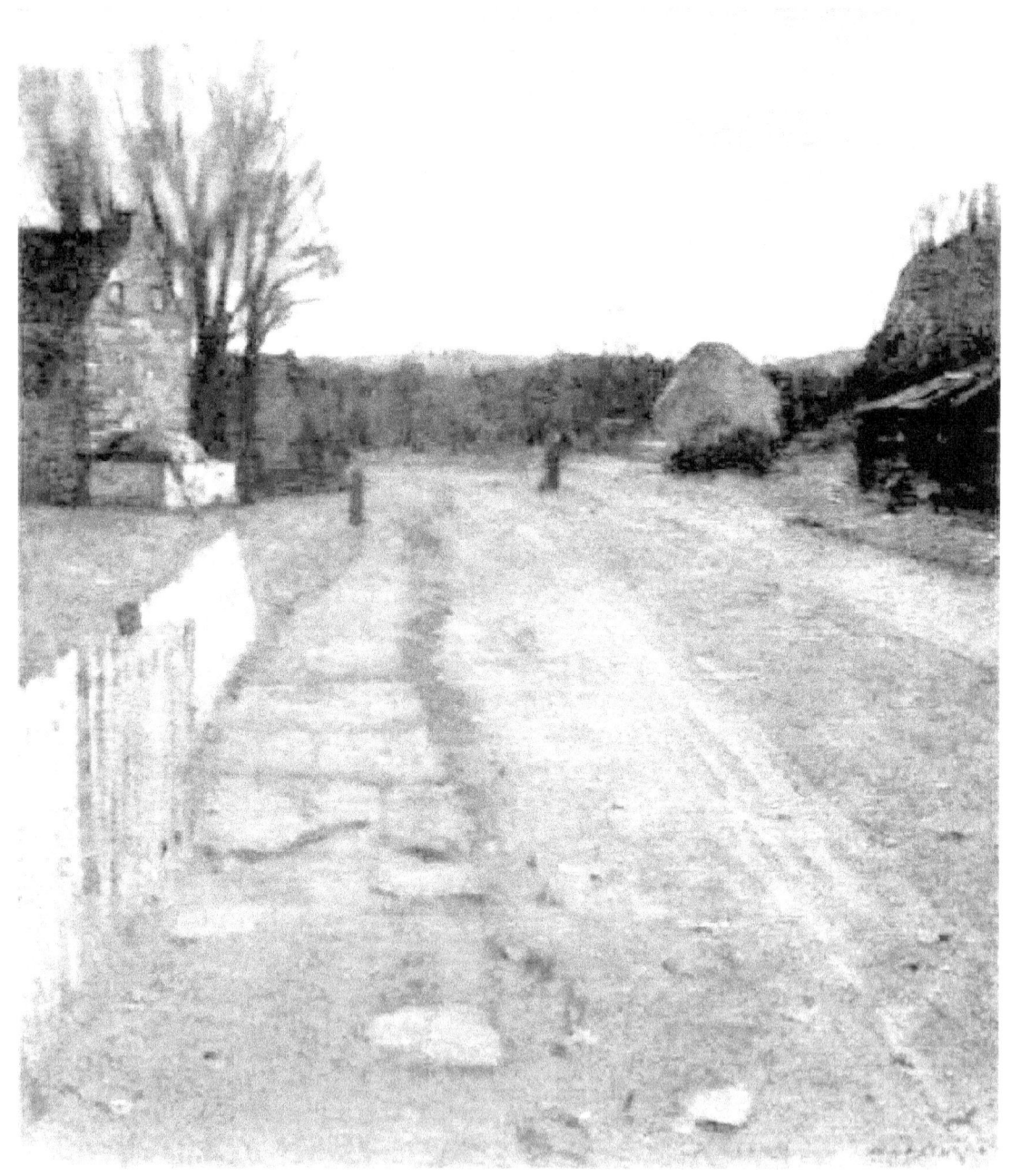

W. L. Lathrop
At Dusk

·XXI·

The Future of American Art

We hear with increasing frequency today the statement that art is universal and without a country; that, being the record of abstract beauty, it cannot be confined within stated geographical limits; that the terms "French art," "English art," etc., are therefore absurd. Art is art *tout bonnement*, and that is all there is to it.

According to these critics, the mere fact that a man with the temperamental sense of beauty chances to be born in France or in Holland does not necessarily make him a French or a Dutch painter. If the Frenchman were brought up in Holland, and the Hollander in France, the Frenchman would then inevitably belong to the Dutch school and the Dutchman would develop as a French impressionist. Each, being temperamentally sensitive to beauty, would simply respond to the appeal of his environment.

Now, if this is correct, there could, of course, be no such thing as American art. But that there is such a thing – an art which would have been impossible but for the evolution of the American man, as distinct from the men of Germany, France, Spain, or even England – is precisely what I hope to demonstrate in this final chapter. And that this American art is destined to grow rapidly in power and distinction, until it occupies for its little time the foremost place in the world of art, is not, I think, beyond the power of reasonable demonstration.

Let us first clear the ground by rehearsing those points upon which both parties are agreed.

All admit, of course, that art is the record of beauty in some one of its myriad forms, be it a Persian rug, a Japanese ceramic, a Greek statue, or a modern oil-painting. In each case, if the beauty be of a sufficiently high order, the result is art. We all admit also that art is personality – that nature is only the crude material from which art is made. This crude material must be fused in the alembic of the human soul, mixed with the alloy of temperament, and colored with the artist's personality before it can be poured out into the final mould and receive the name of art. It is the artist's personality, in other words, that makes the art. And just according to the beauty or the individuality of his temperament will be the beauty or the individuality of the artistic result. If he be a poet, like Corot, the result will be a poetic and delicate interpretation of nature. If he be a colorist, like Monticelli, the result will be some such gorgeous mosaic of splendid color as that wonderful painter gave us. If he be a purist of the fine, clean-cut intellectual type, such as Saint-Gaudens, the result will be something akin to the Sherman monument that dignifies the entrance to Central Park in New York.

But just here comes the dividing line between the contending factions. *What is personality?* One group declares that personality is simply temperament which plays freely within the artist's soul; and, working upon whatever chance material its environment affords, transmutes this crude material into the fine gold of art. The opposing group, while admitting that the basis of artistic personality is temperament, asserts that this temperament is bound hand and foot by the inherited traits and characteristics of a thousand ancestors, and that the Frenchman brought up in Holland would therefore always remain essentially a Frenchman, in spite of his Dutch surroundings. They claim also that racial personality is just as important a factor in all good art as individual personality. They assert, moreover, that no artist can possibly shake off the racial chains that bind him, and that any attempt to do so could only result in some monstrous hybrid or some feeble imitation not deserving the name of art.

Each artist is, first of all, a unit of some specified human group or race. Therefore, if he truly and conscientiously records his own impressions, he will also record the accumulated impressions of the race to which he belongs. That he does this is amply proved by the fact that any reasonably expert judge will tell you whether a picture belongs to the French or the Dutch or the Scandinavian school, without knowing the name of the painter, or anything more of the picture than the canvas itself discloses.

It is impossible, therefore, to avoid the conclusion that racial individuality in art is fact – and a very real and solid fact at that. In some of our modern schools of painting, this racial character is so strong as quite to dominate and submerge the individual note, so that it is often difficult to distinguish the work of one well-known painter from that of some equally celebrated fellow-artist. This is particularly true of the Dutch school, for instance. In fact, the whole art of the Netherlands is so intensely "Dutch" that we may know the characteristics of the Dutch people as well by studying their art as by reading all that has been written about them.

Now, it is a curious thing that, while we in America have, for the past twenty years, been discussing the question of whether any such thing as a national school of art exists here, in Paris "l'Ecole Américaine" has for fully as long a time been recognized as a distinct school, with a marked personal note of its own. And it must be remembered that this verdict was based upon a very partial and imperfect knowledge of American art even as it then existed; for the "American School," as it was known to the French writers of 1885, embraced only a certain number of young American artists who were living in France, and whose whole art training had been received in Paris under exclusively French influences. In spite of this fact, the French critics felt in the work of Sargent, of John Alexander, of Melchers, of Alexander Harrison and of Saint-Gaudens, an exotic note, a new point of view, whose chief characteristic was an unusual directness and clarity of vision, coupled with a corresponding simplicity of statement.

A great French painter once said to me: "You Americans have one advantage over all others. You have no traditions. You can look straight at nature out of your own eyes, while our vision is clouded and obscured by the inheritance of a thousand years."

If to the above list of names we add a few others – Winslow Homer, Homer Martin, John La Farge, George Inness, Alexander H. Wyant, all those of painters who were at that time at the full height of their powers, but who were established at home on this side of the Atlantic – it will be seen that the French were not mistaken in announcing the appearance on the Western horizon of a new and original school of art.

Since the date above mentioned, art in America has made such rapid strides that a roll-call of American artists of the first class taken today would have to include three or four times as many names as could have been mustered in 1885. And it is a significant fact that this increase in the number of American artists, and in the quality of their output, has been coincident with a phenomenal decrease in the number of really great artists at present practising abroad. This decrease has been particularly marked in France, which, during the larger part of the nineteenth century, certainly led the world in all matters connected with art. Yet in France today we will search in vain for any such body of painters as made up the wonderful school of Barbizon, which, in the fifty years beginning with 1830 and ending with 1880, gave the world the greatest art it has seen since the Italian, Dutch, and Spanish Renaissance of the sixteenth century.

It could hardly be expected, I suppose, that this glorious time of blossom and fruitage should repeat itself in France during our own time. Indeed, all history has shown that things do not so happen in the domain of art. Art is a plant whose seed germinates only under certain special and favoring conditions. These conditions are really epochal in their character, and they rarely recur in the life of any one nation; or, if by some specially happy chance they do repeat themselves, it is only after the lapse of many centuries.

To every energetic people there comes sooner or later a time of great material prosperity; it may be as the result of successful wars, of territorial expansion or of commercial supremacy. Whatever the cause, this period of prosperity is invariably accompanied by a tremendous mental stir and awakening, and this, in turn, is followed by a magnificent outburst of art, which lasts for fifty, or maybe a hundred years, and dies away as it came.

Now, if ever in the history of the world conditions have been ripe for the birth of a great art movement, they are so in America today. Titanic forces have been at work for a century preparing the way, extracting untold wealth from a virgin soil; increasing this wealth an hundredfold by the help of marvellous scientific and mechanical genius; conquering, with the irresistible impulse of a new people, every physical obstacle that lay in their way, and building up the richest and most powerful community the world has ever known. Its early struggles are now apparently over, and its surplus wealth is daily increasing. The average of comfort is high and the physical well-being of the people seems practically assured. Whenever in the course of history a nation attains to this stage of development, it begins to reach out toward the ideal, to demand more of life and better than simple food and shelter.

This is precisely what is taking place in America today. There is a growing demand for beauty in all its forms; for the adornment of our public buildings; – for galleries of paintings and statuary, for museums containing porcelains, bronzes, textiles, prints and objects of art of all kinds – a demand so insistent that our municipalities and our legislatures are everywhere beginning to respond to the call of the people. This movement, which may be said to have started a scant ten years ago, is spreading rapidly all over the country. To the art museums in cities of the first class, such as New York, Philadelphia, Boston, Chicago, Cincinnati, and St. Louis, have already been added museums or regular yearly exhibitions in many cities of the second or third class. Among these may be mentioned Pittsburg, Worcester, Buffalo, Toledo, Minneapolis, Kansas City, Atchison, Richmond, Charleston, Atlanta, Memphis, Oakland, and Seattle; while every year a number of names is added to the list. Unless all signs fail, therefore, we may expect during the current century an unprecedented demand for art in the United States, and we are certainly justified in assuming that native artists of the first rank will arise to meet the demand.

Conceding this much, it will be interesting, and also I think quite possible, to forecast the general trend of the movement and the general character of the new art – for new it is bound to be.

If the American painters of thirty years ago had been separated into two groups, the figure-painters on one side and the landscape men on the other, the balance would have been found to be fairly even. If the same thing were repeated today, fully two-thirds of our ablest painters would be found in the camp of the landscapists. This shifting of the balance is most significant, for it shows a new drift, a tendency on the part of our artists to carry their easels out into the open; to paint, or to try to paint, all of the shimmering, iridescent effects that happen only under the great blue arch of the sky; the glory of the noonday sunlight, the pale beauty of the dawn, the golden glow of sunset and the brooding mystery of night.

Why, we may ask, this change of direction? The answer is simple: the artists have discovered that most of the unsolved problems of art lie in the open air. They know by instinct that art, to be alive, must move ever forward toward some new goal. If it remains in one rut, it stagnates or dies. The end of every great art movement has come when its living, rushing, turbulent waters have been congealed into icy formulas – rules of thumb by the use of which the mere artisan can produce a sort of "near-art" which is necessarily without vitality or charm. The true artist must always be an innovator, a pioneer in fresh fields, an adventurer seeking new Eldorados. If he now goes afield, therefore, it is because he knows that in the domain of indoor figure painting there are few undiscovered countries. This branch of art was exploited long ago by the old masters, and their achievements were so transcendent that any modem painter who sets out to equal or excel them in their own chosen line must be endowed with a large share of courage and self-confidence.

Another cause of this universal return to nature is doubtless the fact that our lives are not, humanly speaking, so beautiful as they once were. Our clothing is no longer picturesque. The advent of farm machinery has destroyed much of the pastoral and bucolic beauty of country life. The sowing and reaping and binding and threshing that were done by hand in the old days with such splendid rhythmic swing of muscle are now matters of revolving wheels and clattering chains and knives. Even our buildings have deteriorated – at least from the artist's point of view; for the comfortable villa farmhouse of the present day does not cling lovingly to the soil and become part of the environing landscape, as did the spreading, low-hung buildings of our fathers. And so, to quench the eternal thirst for beauty, we must needs return once more to kindly nature, whose beauty is exhaustless and everlasting. Her skies have lost none of their early crystalline charm of color; her hills and her rock-bound coasts are as grand as ever; her trees, her rivers and her spreading fields are as beautiful and as appealing now as in the days of Hesiod. But, precious beyond all other things, her exquisite and ever-varying effects – that happen because of the change from night to day and from day to night again – are spread out always before us, an endless feast of beauty for those who have eyes to see and minds to appreciate.

Nevertheless, it is quite possible that, in the very changed conditions of our civilization, there may lurk wonderful and hitherto unsuspected opportunities for our future artists, and especially our figure-painters. There is certainly a strange picturesqueness in some of our modern steel mills, with their cyclopean forces at work against backgrounds of whirling steam and glowing furnace. Even our skyscrapers have an unusual beauty of their own, and the skyline of lower New York is far from being ugly or uninteresting. Another field that is replete with possibilities is the teeming and kaleidoscopic life of our city slums, which the inexorable law of migration has crowded with strange peoples from the far corners of the earth; peoples who are as yet unassimilated, who still wear their exotic costumes and live their strange, foreign lives in our very midst. There has already been some attempt to use this exhaustless material (unfortunately, as yet, without adequate technical skill), but when the trained master shall paint for us the life of our streets with all its vital and original character, we shall welcome his pictures as a priceless addition to the world's store of precious things.

I have as yet made no mention of mural painting, which is, of course, destined to occupy a very important place in the art of the future. Thousands of new public and private buildings all over the country will call for decoration, and I have no hesitation in predicting that the opportunity thus afforded will result in some bewilderingly great discovery in advance of our present-day knowledge of that art – a step in advance at least as important as that made by Puvis de Chavannes when he painted the out-of-door atmosphere upon the walls of the Panthéon in Paris. It is at least certain that the movement in this same direction will be pushed much farther than at present, and that open-air effects and open-air tones will be used with increasing frequency by our mural painters, because on this line only can they hope to achieve any notable advance over their predecessors.

The fact is that the open has claimed us as a people! We devote ourselves with ever-increasing enthusiasm to out-of-door pleasures and out-of-door pursuits; we have learned to love out-of-door nature and out-of-door beauty. It is our best achievement as a nation; and our artists in this are, therefore, simply keeping step with the march of modern civilization.

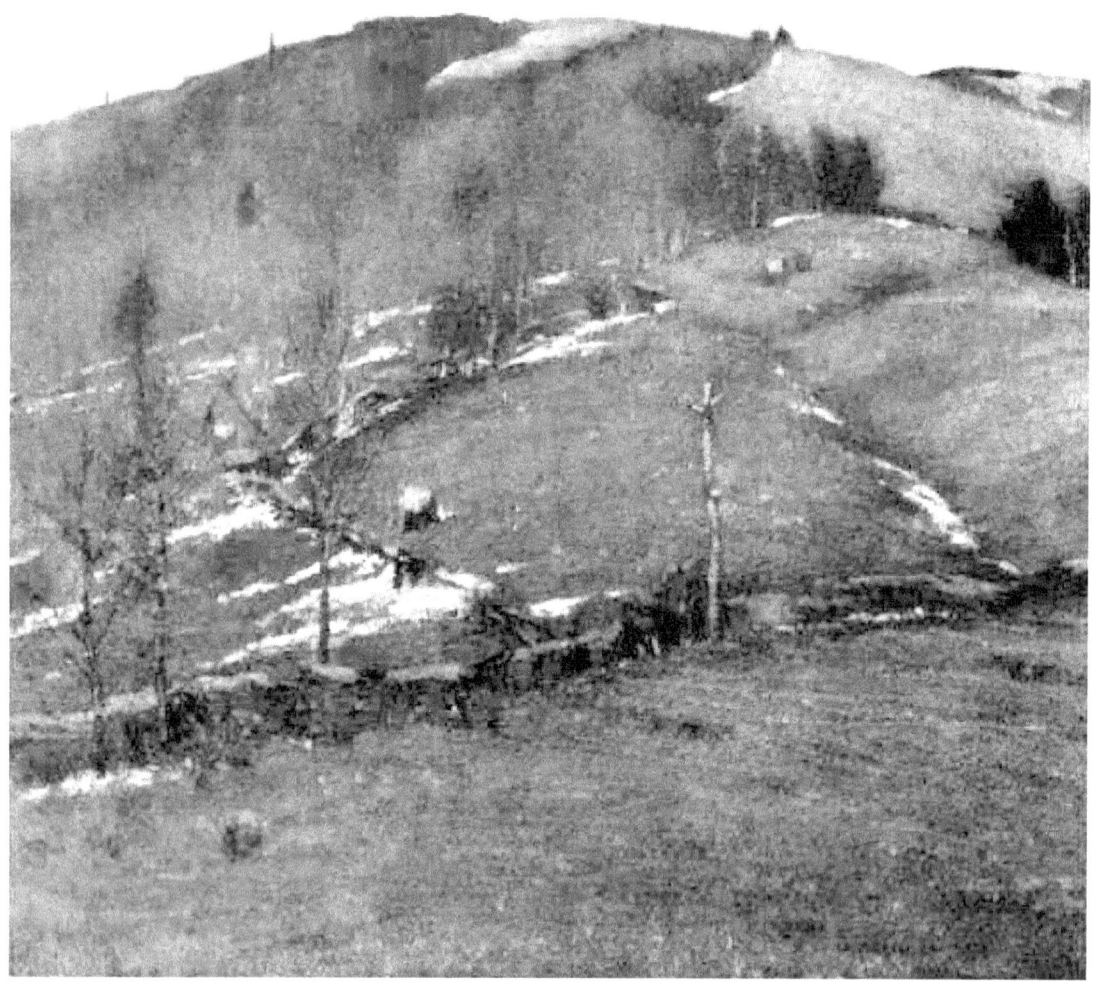

Bruce Crane
November Hills

Bibliography

The Hudson Rover School - General
The Hudson River School: Nature and the American Vision
by the New York Historical Society and Linda S. Ferber
©2009

American Wilderness: The Story of the Hudson River School of Painting
by Barbara Babcock Millhouse
©2007

The Hudson River School: The Landscape Art of Bierstadt, Cole, Church, Durand, Heade and Twenty Other Artists
by Louise Minks
©1999

American Paradise: The World of the Hudson River School
by Ken Avery
©1987

The Hudson River School - Artists
The American Landscapes of Asher B. Durand (1796-1886)
by Linda S. Ferber, Barbara Novak and Barbara Dayer
©2011

Kindred Spirits: Asher B. Durand and the American Landscape
by Linda Ferber
©2007

Hudson River School Visions: The Landscapes of Sanford R. Gifford
by Ken Avery and Franklin Kelly
©2003

John Frederick Kensett: An American Master
by John Paul Driscoll and John K. Howat
©1985

Frederic Church
by John K. Howat
©2005

Frederic Edwin Church: Romantic Landscapes and Seascapes
by Gerald L. Carr
©2008

Frederic Church and the Landscape Oil Sketch
by Andrew Wilton
©2013

Frederic E. Church: Under Changing Skies : Oil Sketches and Drawings from the Collection of the Cooper-Hewitt Museum
by Elaine Evans Dee
©1992

To Embrace the Universe: The Drawings of Frederic Edwin Church
by Elaine Evans Dee
©1984

Precursors to Tonalism
John Constable and the Theory of Landscape Painting
by Ray Lambert
©2004

The Intimate Landscape: A New Look at the Origins of the American Barbizon Movement
by Estelle Riback
©2004

Corot in Italy: Open-Air Painting and the Classical-Landscape Tradition
by Peter Galassi
©1996

In the Light of Italy: Corot and Early Open-Air Painting
by Philip Conisbee, Sarah Faunce and Jeremy Strick
©1996

Tonalism - General
A History of American Tonalism, 1880-1920
by David Adams Cleveland
©2010

Poetic Vision: American Tonalism
by Ralph Sessions
©2005

Like Breath on Glass: Whistler, Inness, and the Art of Painting Softly
by Marc Simpson
©2008

Tonalism - Artists
George Inness and the Visionary Landscape
by Adrienne Baxter Bell
©2007

George Inness and the Science of Landscape
by Rachael Ziady DeLue
©2007

Landscape Painting - Instruction
Landscape Painting
by Adrian Scott Stokes
©1925

Carlson's Guide to Landscape Painting
by John F. Carlson
©1973

Other artbooks and DVDs currently available from Velatura Press

Memory Drawing: Perceptual Training and Recall by Darren R. Rousar
All drawing and painting from life is at some point done from memory, even if that memory is only seconds old. An artist's ability to recall something previously seen is all the more important when their subject is no longer in view. Da Vinci, Corot, Degas, Whistler, and Inness wrote about it. In fact, Inness claimed that many of his best landscape paintings were done from memory. *Memory Drawing: Perceptual Training and Recall* teaches you how to visually perceive and accurately recall those perceptions. It will also help you improve your abilities to remember fleeting effects, seize essentials, and even enhance your imagination.

Cast Drawing Using the Sight-Size Approach by Darren R. Rousar
The first book of its kind, *Cast Drawing Using the Sight-Size Approach* teaches the student a systematic way to meet the challenges of drawing. Traditionally taught in classical art ateliers, sight-size is an approach to drawing and painting from life. It is through cast drawing that the basics of sight-size are learned. This approach is readily adaptable to other disciplines such as portraiture, still life, interiors, landscape, figurative painting and sculpture.

Cast Painting Using the Sight-Size Approach by Darren R. Rousar
After cast drawing, cast painting is the next step for the student at many classical art ateliers, *Cast Painting Using the Sight-Size Approach* provides the student with all of the necessary information to succeed at sight-size cast painting in oil. In addition to teaching the theory and processes involved in cast painting, *Cast Painting Using the Sight-Size Approach* also has sections on materials and stretching canvas as well as a short commentary on the "unity of effect," with selections from R. A. M. Stevenson's 1895 edition of *Velasquez*.

Sight-Size and the Art of Seeing by Darren R. Rousar
For those who prefer to be taught through sight and sound, the DVD *Sight-Size and the Art of Seeing* presents the complete cast drawing instruction described in its companion volume, *Cast Drawing Using the Sight-Size Approach*. Also on the DVD is a section discussing some of the history of sight-size.

Drawing Made Easy with Selections from Practical Drawing by E. G. Lutz
Once a classic drawing instruction manual that was used to teach countless children and young adults how to draw, *Drawing Made Easy* by E. G. Lutz is now back in print after many years absence. Hallmarks of his approach are simplifying complex shapes as well as working from big to small. These concepts, outlined in *Drawing Made Easy*, are simple enough for children to understand and yet the same principles are evident in many Old Master drawings. Also contained within this reprinted volume are selections from Lutz's earlier book, *Practical Drawing*.

All books and DVDs are sold through Amazon and other online booksellers

www.ingramcontent.com/pod-product-compliance
Lightning Source LLC
Chambersburg PA
CBHW080916170526
45158CB00008B/2135